Dead Girls Don't Die©

By Elliot M. Rubin

Copyright February 24, 2017
United States Library of Congress
ISBN 10 #0-9981796-0-4
ISBN 13 # 978-0-9981796-0-5

Acknowledgements

I would like to thank my father, Herman S. Rubin z"l for his inspiration and encouragement to write.

He wrote essays, prayers, and poetry his whole life and his writings are treasured by those who have read them.

Also, I would like to thank my beloved grandmother, Bessie Greenberg. Her lunchtime stories of Moishe Kapoya when I was a child stirred my creative mind to picture the story, and think.

And finally I want to thank my dear wife Laura who is an avid reader, and whose encouragement to write is most appreciated.

Chapter One

The little girl is visibly following through the glass doors to the street her father and older brother as they walk out of the store. With no warning, she views their bodies shake, fall to their knees, and sprawl out on the concrete seemingly lifeless. A blood-curdling scream emanates from the depths of her soul and shatters the store's quiet hum as her mother raises her head to glimpse at half her family lying on the sidewalk motionless.

Moments preceding them leaving the showroom the little girl is clutching her new look-alike Miss USA Baby Doll and smiling from cheek to cheek. The young girl is holding the toy close to her chest while she grasped onto her mother's dress the two began to prepare to leave.

The family from the cornfields of the Midwest is visiting New York City for the first time and is about to exit the custom doll store. The father walks out first grasping her ten-year-old brother's hand the little girl sneezes causing the mother to stop, and stand to the side taking out a facial tissue to wipe the young girl's nose. The people behind them continue to walk by and head for the exit.

Only a precious few minutes before a white cargo van with no logos on the side completely stopped in the middle of a busy Broadway at Forty-Ninth Street causing traffic to back up. Cars started blowing their horns nonstop with a New York attitude. Drivers opened their windows, and expletives are hurled at the vehicle tying up the flow of southbound traffic flow.

A quick flip up and the van's darkened glass top hatch opens. Two hands rise out of the opening, and place a drone on the roof panels then disappears back inside sealing the vehicle. Within a few seconds, the remote-controlled aircraft flies vertically up and hovers about thirty feet in midair.

An immediate right turn onto the side street allows the white van to create distance away from the hovering aircraft and comes to a full stop near the Hudson River. From the front of the truck, the driver can operate the small aircraft via a joystick and a smartphone by using a penlight camera attached to the top of the tiny whirling motors

The drone is treading air over Broadway then starts flying south toward the pedestrian mall in Times Square, and releases a refined powder mixing in with the fumes of congested New York City traffic below.

The wind carries the substance to the innocents on the street beneath as they inhale the toxin, and begin to lose their breath. One by one men, women and children start to shake and fall on the hard concrete sidewalk not moving. The mounted police feel their horses start to sway, the legs of their sturdy mounts buckle, and collapse to the street trapping the dying officers beneath.

From one side of Times Square to the other the drone careens like a pinball spraying its poisoned cargo over the mass of humanity.

Pedestrians run in all directions as panic sets in seeing others die in front of their eyes. The harder they breathe while running the more they take a deep breath into their gasping lungs. No one understands what is happening as they see other people fall into the ground and not moving, yet no one glances up to the sky.

Hundreds are lying flat on the pavement as vehicles with their windows closed are still able to continue driving through the area. Suddenly one by one the cars and trucks stop, people stepping out to help, and they too inhale the deadly toxic air. In a few minutes, the downtown flowing traffic comes to a complete halt and backs up as far north as Columbus Circle.

Automobiles with unconscious drivers are rumbling out of control over fallen bodies and come crashing onto the sidewalks, and into storefronts.

At the NASDAQ building, a CNBC show is live on the air, and the panel stops talking. Silence prevails as the commentators begin to stare through the immense sidewalk windows at what is happening on the pedestrian plaza.

The New York City technical manager of operations for CNBC is at the studio, and orders the cameras turned to face Times Square to capture what is going on outside. Through the earpieces instructions are given all doors are to stay shut, and a camera crew is sent to the second floor inside balcony to obtain a high shot of Times Square. Someone calls 911 on their mobile phone to report hundreds of people are lying on the sidewalk, and not moving.

Nobody at the time of the terror attack observes anything flying over the people on the ground. All eyes are on the huge number of motionless people on the street covering the plaza and streets like a blanket of human bodies.

The drone turns west onto Forty-Second Street while continuing to release the toxic spray as it heads for the Hudson River to meet with the nondescript white truck.

As it approaches the water the van driver directs the flying angle of death away and flies it out to sea. With care, the aircraft goes under the Verrazano Bridge heading east and eventually falls into the depths of the Atlantic Ocean when its fuel runs out. No one is going to be able to find it, or trace it back to the terrorist once it sinks to the ocean floor.

The van driver believes it is the perfect terror crime, and turns north heading for the Cross Bronx Expressway, and exits off by Hunts Point. The vehicle is parked, the keys left in it with the doors open. The probability is high tonight someone will commit an auto theft, and is going to steal the van of death, and will be caught sooner or later. No traces of ownership will be able to be found, and fingerprints wiped clean. The car thieves will take the rap if caught.

Sirens are blaring in the canyons of tall buildings as police cars and ambulances converge at Times Square. The Hazardous Materials Rescue (HMR) Unit No. 1 from Queens is summoned to Midtown. The middle of Manhattan is cordoned off, and no one is allowed to enter the area or leave their buildings until the EPA determines what unknown is killing people.

The governor, visiting the city this day for a political meeting, is taken to the city's emergency control center to warn people to stay indoors. HMR Unit 1 uses a computer which can determine what kind of poison is being used. Surprisingly to everyone's chagrin, there are no traces of a toxin which can be found once they arrive on the scene. Only the hundreds of autopsies will find out what destroyed so many lives today.

The Federal Environmental Protection Agency is called in to assist. Their white clean protective suits are being worn, and due to Federal budget cuts, not enough qualified staff is available to handle all the dead people involved. The city's morgue is overburdened, and bodies are placed in sealed body bags and taken to private funeral homes in all the boroughs where extra refrigerated units to store them are maintained and used.

***

In a rush to get down the building's staircase Khara first needs to disassemble her sniper rifle, and place it in her backpack. With no hesitation, she takes off her dark blue hoodie, rolls it up into a tight ball, places it on the top of the bag, and puts on a bright pink one with a white baseball cap to change her appearance. A different look is needed in case someone saw her on the roof with a rifle aiming at the presidential candidate Congressman Ted Ferry. Nobody saw a person in a pink outfit on the roof of the building.

Mayhem breaks out in the crowd of attendees when the candidate is shot dead on the steps of City Hall as he is starting to give a speech. The mayor, by standing next to Congressman Ted Ferry is in shock as the congressman's blood splatters all over his light tan suit.

The Secret Service agents draw their weapons, and with the sun in their eyes, they are having difficulty looking around to see where the gunshot came from. The sniper rifle is relatively quiet as the recoil noise cannot be heard as Khara used a sound suppressor so no echo from the gun bounces off the canyon of tall buildings. The shooting only took her seconds to aim, fire, and hustle off the rooftop from where she made the fatal shot.

With a grip of steel, she holds on the brass railings of the old building while she bounds down the stairs until she reaches the fourth floor. The stairwell exit door is opened and she starts walking the hallways searching for a ladies room. Upon finding it she enters, goes into the last stall, closes the metal door, and locks it from the inside.

In one swift move, she takes off the backpack, hangs it on the hook inside the door, takes out fast drying metal epoxy, and glues the sliding locking door bolt shut. With both hands, she reaches up, grabs the side of the stall at the top, and pulls herself up and over into the next stall. In her pocket, she takes out a small container of axle grease which she smears on the underside of the stall's walls, and on the top ledges. The dirty looking substance will appear to people as if someone defecated, and wiped it on the stall. No one will be willing to touch it to find out otherwise and will leave her backpack alone. In a day or two, she will come back and retrieve her rifle from the locked stall.

After leaving the building she is standing on the corner of Broadway directly across from City Hall Park when she hears sirens approaching. EMT ambulances are rushing to help the candidate.

People on the street are yelling there is a shooting by the park. No one is sure who is shot or where, but the electricity of danger is in the air as crowds start to panic.

Now Khara can walk unencumbered on the street, and take the subway back uptown to visit Eloise in the hospital. With a transit pass in hand she swipes the card, pays the fare and now she is standing on the station platform waiting for an express train. The rush of air preceding the train feels good on her face as it cools off the beads of sweat resulting from her walking down fifteen flights of stairs and climbing over the restroom partition.

The subway arrives and stops in front of her as she steps in and as usual stands by the rear door in the car. This enables her to see who walks on, and what is happening if anything, while the train is moving.

In a few minutes the train reaches her station, she gets off and walks the rest of the way to the hospital to be with Eloise who is recovering from a heart attack.

The security guard at the entrance recognizes her from the other day when she arrived to see Eloise, and Khara wave's hello. The man only came on duty a few minutes before she arrived, and she said entering the building and walking by him "I needed some fresh air; I can't stand being inside here all night." The guard nodded a knowing yes and turned to greet the next person walking in. If need be he will be her eyewitness she was in the hospital all night.

The door to the room is open, she walks back into Eloise's room, and she is amazed how many wires and oxygen tubes are still attached to her body. The pale green walls impart a dulling effect. Tired Khara sits in a large tan vinyl chair, starts to close her eyes when a nurse walks in and asks how she slept, trying to be friendly. "These chairs are not great for sleeping in," Khara said.

Luck is an important thing to possess.

Due to the extreme causality numbers from Times Square, the whole hospital is in overdrive. Due to the emergency if a patient is not in cardiac distress the nurses are ignoring them and running down to the emergency room to try to help out. The ambulances can't keep up with the bodies being brought into the hospital. Sadly they fail to revive any of the victims who were brought to this day.

Therefore as far as everyone is concerned Khara spent two days sitting next to the bedside of her psychiatrist, and part-time lover.

In the quiet of the intensive care unit, Khara starts to relax and closes her eyes for a moment or two. Her phone, being silenced starts to buzz in her pocket, and she takes it out to see who is calling. The readout says it is her supervisor.

Johanna is the Assistant New York City Police Commissioner in charge of terrorism, her direct supervisor, and also part-time lover. In her mind, Khara thinks she is calling about the shooting a few hours go at City Hall, but she is not.

"Khara where are you?"

"Today I'm visiting my psychiatrist in the hospital. She had a heart attack, and I've been here for two days, why?"

"Have you watched any television or listened to the radio?"

"No they don't turn on the television in ICU, why, what's going on?"

"Today a terrorist attack took place in Times Square in the late morning. No one is aware yet who is behind this but almost one thousand people have been killed. I am sorry to say no one survived. People who were out on the street died; only the ones who stayed inside buildings are still alive. We are trying to find out how this happened. Can you can meet me at the police substation on Times Square in one hour, it would be helpful?"

"Okay, I'll be on my way immediately."

The call with Johanna ends as Eloise opens her eyes, and smiles when she realizes who is sitting by her bedside.

"Please Khara hold my hand, I'm so glad to see you here."

"Where else would I be? I've been here a long time watching you."

A psychopathic killer harbors no hesitation in telling a lie, even to her shrink if it helps build her alibi. Not sure she will need it, but in the future, she may need one.

"Maybe when I feel better maybe we can go on another cruise together like we did before, what do you say Khara?"

"A cruise with you would be wonderful. You need to be better first. Unfortunately, I must go now the assistant police commissioner called me. She encountered a major problem in Times Square, and I have to travel up there to meet her. Hopefully, I will be able to return to you later if I can."

Still holding Khara's hand Eloise smiles, pulls her close to her, and kisses her goodbye.

Being a very independent person, also a self-acknowledged Adrenalin junkie, Khara values Eloise's judgment, and for decades has used her as a valued sounding board.

***

Later when Khara walks out of the hospital she spots a squad car stopped for a traffic light. With an attitude, she walks in front of the car and flashes her gold detective's badge.

"Can you take me to the sub-precinct on the Square I need to go uptown to Broadway and Seventh Avenue in Times Square for a meeting with the assistant commissioner?"

The tone of her voice sounded more like an authoritative command than a question.

The officer driving waves her over to the side of the car and inspects her identification before he lets her in. With lights flashing and siren blaring they are on their way.

Times Square is still blocked off, and only emergency services personnel are allowed into the area. The HMR Unit 1 and the Federal EPA people have declared it safe to walk through the area although they are still doing tests. The lab unit determined no toxic residue can be found anywhere on the ground.

The police car is allowed to drive into the area, and they drop her off at the police substation in Times Square. Khara exits the car as Johanna who is standing on the sidewalk waiting spots Khara and calls out for her to come inside.

Both of them walk into the substation, and Khara recognizes her fiancé Don Weber is standing and reading a police report. Since he is an FBI terrorism expert stationed in New York he is called in on this case. Meeting again in the station when they see each other they embrace and quickly kiss.

"Hey, Khara did Johanna fill you in on what happened in Times Square and Forty-Second Street all the way west to the Hudson River?"

"No, but the cops who drove me down here told me hundreds of people were killed. Do you know what caused it yet?"

"The lab guys are puzzled. There is no trace on the ground or on anything else in the area. The Feds believe this has to be a biological toxin; they cannot think of any other logical answer. The commissioner requested the autopsy reports on the first victims brought in to try to secure a better handle on what caused this mess, and I am waiting for it to arrive."

With her right hand, she opens the door and Khara walks outside then glances at the light posts in Times Square. The memory of the explosion in front of her apartment house recently comes to mind as she remembers seeing cameras on top of the lamp posts. Olga had set them up illegally so her security team could keep an eye on the street in front of their headquarters in Brooklyn.

Midtown is full of cameras, both police and privately owned.

Johanna follows her outside leaving him in the substation.

"Has anyone looked at the videos yet from all the cameras in the area?"

"The department is gathering the private tapes from the surrounding buildings plus their own videos

and will be looking at them as soon as possible"
Johanna said.

"Smart move, I wonder what they will find out."

"Time will tell Khara. Did you hear about Ted
Ferry being assassinated today about the same time this
happened here? Where were you when he was killed, or
shouldn't I ask?"

"You can ask me I don't mind. For two days I
was with my psychiatrist in the hospital. She had a
heart attack, and I stayed with her until you called me.
There are witnesses at the hospital who can tell you I
was sitting with her all night."

"To be honest with you I don't care or give a
damn. The man was a piece of human shit, and I'm glad
he is gone. At any rate, the country doesn't need a drug-
dealing racist as president."

"Listen, Johanna, if something comes up let me
know. There is not much I can do here at the moment.
Later I'm going home."

Walking back a few steps she opens the station
door and calls into Don. "I'm leaving now, when are
you finished?"

"Give me a second and I'll be done too Khara,
do you want to come back to my place with me
tonight?"

"Okay let's go, we'll have to walk a few blocks
east to grab a cab. No traffic is allowed in Times Square
yet unless it is an emergency vehicle."

"Sounds like a plan, I'm ready."

Both walk out of the substation holding hands
and head toward the East River where they hope to hail
a cab and hop in the back seat.

"Take us uptown to Washington Heights," he
said.

"Don it's late, before we go to your place do you
feel like something to eat?"

"What do you have in mind Khara?"

"Driver do you know where Egan's Bar and Grill is?"

The cab driver overhears the conversation and has a question for them.

"Do you want me to drive to Egan's instead, I eat there a lot? The food is good."

"Yes, they should still be open, it is only late afternoon and I haven't been back since I was transferred to Staten Island. Take us to Egan's please."

It is not too long until the taxi stops in front of Egan's, and Don and Khara scamper out of the vehicle and into the bar.

Apple Street is dark due to the tall buildings. Located in an old former industrial area near the Hudson River the bar at first glance appears gloomy.

"Egan's appears to be a dive bar Khara, you actually eat here?"

"Don't worry, the food is great, and you can stare at the blond waitress' boobs all afternoon. The waitress always opens a few buttons on her blouse to entice you to leave a bigger tip."

Being old school he opens the door to the bar for her to enter first, and they walk into the sound of a Jukebox playing "Do you love me" by the Contours. The lighting is dim, the bar is almost full with the after-work crowd, and a few tables are still available.

The waitress walks up to Khara and gives her a wry smile. "Welcome back honey, want your usual table? It's open at the moment."

"Yes, the table in the rear will be fine."

"Good, you know where it is, I have to pick up a bar order so I'll be back. Go seat yourself."

"C'mon follow me we have a table in the back."

Leading him by the hand they walk through the packed bar past full tables to the rear of the place to the last one. The chair against the wall is pulled out so when sitting her back is to the wall, and she faces the entrance, Khara looks up waiting at Don for him to sit.

The place is packed, and he is still standing glancing around at the people with a quizzical look on his face like why am I here?

"Don't worry you can sit its clean. The place is old and looks unsanitary, but the food is good. Look at the sidewall for today's menu on your left, and behind the bar. Whatever you order is made fresh, and delicious. Egan himself is as a rule in the back cooking his late wife's recipes."

Finally, he pulls out his chair and sits after tilting it so some crumbs fall off onto the floor.

The waitress walks over and places her hands flat on the table, tilts her head upward and pushes her chest out. The top few buttons of her blouse are open and ample cleavage is protruding ready to burst forth and escape.

"What'll you have to drink?"

Although Khara normally drinks Amstel Light tonight she orders a twenty-ounce glass of Heineken on tap. "I'll have the same please," Don said.

"Thanks, I'll be right back with your drinks."

"So what are you eating today Khara? Wait a minute I am reading a few items written on the wall I might like."

"If you are hungry I recommend the Hungarian beef goulash. Egan makes it fresh almost daily, and it is his late wife's recipe. Turn around and look at the cash register behind the bar you will find a picture of her leaning against the mirror next to it."

"I think so, the goulash sounds good to me, and I can see the picture now."

"Sometimes when the time is short and I'm in a hurry I usually order it. His cheeseburgers are fantastic but they are rolled, cooked to order, and takes a while. The goulash though is simmering all day long. After a lot of the food is served and the pot gets too low he cooks up a fresh batch. Tonight I'm hungry so I am going to order it, try it, you will enjoy it."

"Okay, we'll both have the goulash too. Tonight I'm going to trust your experience eating in this place."

The waitress brings over their drinks, and again places her hands on the table, twists her upper torso to face Don, and asks him "what would you like tonight?"

His face is now at eye level with her chest, and his eyes are forced stare at it trying to burst out of a bra a size or two too small.

"Please bring me what Khara is ordering, thanks."

With a wry smile at him, she now stands erect and turns to face Khara.

"We'll both have the goulash, and a few rolls also for the leftover gravy."

"Okay, I'll put the order it. Give me a few minutes, and I'll be back with the bread and setups."

After the waitress walks away Don extends his hand across the table, places it over Khara's, and asks her a question.

"Did you give any thought about where and when we can go to be married?"

"Yes, I gave it a lot of thought. My problem is your promotion and transfer to the Midwest. Honestly, I don't know if I can live in Middle America. The area may be too quiet for me."

The truth of the matter is she has not discussed it yet in depth with Eloise. The first marriage ended after she sent her husband to the hospital for the umpteenth time, and she is hesitant to be in a committed relationship like a marriage again. This excuse is a stalling tactic, not a definite negative answer.

"Well, nothing about the advancement and transfer is done yet Khara. There is always the option I could stay here at my current grade level, and pass the promotion up. For you, I would be willing to do anything."

"Listen, Don, I do want to marry you. To be ho9nest with you I need a little more time. Remember I said when you gave me the ring I have issues you know nothing about. Now I need to speak to my psychiatrist but she is in the hospital from a heart attack. As soon as she gets out I'll make an appointment, and discuss it in depth with her. Listen I promise you I will."

Leaning over the table she plants a lingering kiss on his lips and wraps her arms around his neck.

"Excuse me I have some hot food here I'd like to put down."

Khara sits back; the waitress places their food on the table and walks away.

"The food sure looks good Khara I can't wait to taste it."

"You'll like it, I always do."

After finishing the meal they wipe up the gravy with a roll and sit back with full stomachs.

"The food was filling, and I would also say great tasting. I am glad I came here with you. When you're ready let's head out, and try to grab a cab to my place."

"I'm ready, let's go."

Don signals for the waitress to come over, and he asks for the check. A credit card is taken out of his wallet, and he gives it to the waitress and waits for his receipt.

When they walk outside it is already evening, and they decide to walk over to the West Side Highway to try to catch a cab. But there is little traffic due to the terrorist attack only a few blocks away. People are staying out of midtown Manhattan due to the embargo on cars entering the area.

"Maybe I'll call a car service Khara. They are always available."

"No, I have a better idea. Only a few blocks north of where we are I know a gentleman's club is located. Taxi cabs are always dropping off men or picking them up. Come on it's a short walk, and I'm still stuffed from dinner."

"How do you know about the club being a few blocks away?"

"Did you forget this used to be my precinct before I was transferred to the old age retirement home on Staten Island they call a police station?"

"Guess I did, and I think I see it up ahead."

Carefully they cross the street, and Don spots two large bouncers standing by the front door inspecting ID's.

Both are heavy-set men, but one is huge.

As they approach closer Khara calls out to the larger of the two men.

"Hey Biggie, are you working here now?"

This massive man turns around, and a smile crosses his face. Without hesitation, he puts his arms out, steps toward Khara, and gives her a hug. Don, standing motionless in wonderment, watches as his fiancé is hugging a huge bouncer the size of a tree outside a strip club. After lifting Khara off her feet he places her down in a gentle manner.

"Biggie I want you to meet my fiancé Don Weber. Don is an FBI Special Agent." This is said to clue Big Boy in so he doesn't say anything about their past murderous adventures together.

"Nice to meet you, Don, I know Khara for a while now. Congratulations and lots of luck."

"Thank you."

Being Khara is curious, and she wants to confirm her suspicions. Big Boy is loyal to her dead boyfriend's crime family. The thinking is Al Junior owns the place, and he is probably working the door for the time being.

"So Junior inherited this club?"

"Yes, he has a manager who used to work for his father running the place in Staten Island. There is a lot of uncertainty if he is going to reopen the Staten Island club. Junior never liked it in Staten Island, but it was convenient for his dad. Al used to hang out at the bar all the time; he felt it was more relaxing than here in Manhattan. The old club was more of a dance club than a strip place where he used to chill out and watch the girls dance. This place is hopping with action and is a lot more interesting for Junior. What are you doing here today anyway?"

"We were called in about the terrorist incident in Times Square, and afterward we went out for dinner. Can you call us a cab? We are going to Washington Heights."

"I'll do you one better than calling a cab for you."

Big Boy reaches in his pocket and takes out his cell phone. "Bring my white Cadillac around. I need to take some people home. Tiny will check ID's until I come back. Hey did you ever meet my cousin Tiny?"

"No never."

"His father is Big Tony and we call him Tiny Tony. Since Al died he is in training with me full time."

Everyone can hear car tires screeching against the asphalt as a Cadillac turns sharply around the corner, and stops in front of Big Boy. A large young man flips the keys to Big Boy, waves hello to everyone, and walks inside the club.

"Want you to know Khara I'm doing you a solid Khara, jump in I'm taking you uptown."

"Thanks, Biggie I appreciate the ride."

Don opens the rear door for Khara and follows her in the back seat. They snap in their seat belts at the same time as Big Boy slams the gas pedal to the floor. The front of the car juts upwards into the air, and races forward burning rubber. The centrifugal force pushes them back into their seats.

Still, curious Khara continues questioning Big Boy.

"How is Junior doing? Is he still running things out of his funeral home in Brooklyn?"

"Yes but not as much as he used to. Junior is running around more now since Al was killed. Are you still in Staten Island?"

"For the moment I am. Soon I'll be transferred back soon to my old precinct in Manhattan."

"It'll be like old times Khara" Big Boy said.

As they approached Washington Heights Don gives him the street number. The car pulls over and drops them off in front of his apartment house.

Both thank him for the lift, and he drives away heading back to the club.

Standing on the sidewalk Don asks her how she knows the bouncer.

"Remember I used to go to the dance club in Staten Island for lunch or dinner a lot. Biggie was the bouncer at the club's door also."

Reaching into his pocket he takes out his keys and starts to unlock the front entrance door. Turning the handle he pushes open the steel and glass door in when a young man in a hoodie appears almost out of nowhere.

"Thanks for holding the door for me mister."

A sixth sense told Khara something is wrong. "Wait a minute, do you live here?"

"Yes on the third floor."

"What is your apartment number? Don asked.

"I live in 3B."

Khara answered him with a sharp tone to her voice.

"No, you don't. Get the hell out of here before I arrest you."

Facing him Khara slides her pink hoodie back by the zipper exposing her gold detective's badge, and her holstered Sig Sauer.

The young man took two steps back, turned, and walked away without saying anything further.

"What an asshole. I was only here once but noticed the apartment numbers are in hundreds. A third-floor apartment would be 301B, not 3B."

"I'm impressed Khara. What else can you do?"

Let's go into your apartment, take a shower together, and I'll show you what else I can do."

Chapter Two

By the next morning, almost all the bodies are removed from Times Square and the only reminder of what occurred are chalk outlines signaling where people fell to the ground. The police are going into every building in the area searching for clues, and additional officers are still buzzing around looking for something, anything, which might give them a lead.

After dressing, Khara and Don walk to the subway to go downtown but first, stop in a coffee shop on the corner of his block to eat a quick breakfast. They sit at the counter, and Don orders first "eggs over easy with toast please." A buttered roll and black coffee are all Khara ever eats in the morning. When finished Don pays the check and they walk to the subway a block away and go downtown to Times Square to continue delving into what occurred.

The forensic investigators from the Federal government and the city's crime lab spent the entire night going over the area, found nothing on the ground, and continued to keep the streets closed off to traffic and the public until they are sure it is safe.

As the two walk up the stairs from the subway tunnel to street level Don kisses Khara goodbye, and heads for his office on the east side of town. Khara continues to the precinct substation where she is expecting to meet Johanna.

Outside the substation which is located in the middle of the square Johanna is waiting and spots Khara crossing the street. A few yards behind her are some of the department's lab men with a detail of law enforcement escorting them. Everybody arrives at the location about the same time.

The lead lab officer approaches Johanna.

"Commissioner we need to ask you to please come with us to headquarters. The President's Secretary of Home Land Security is waiting for you in your office. We need to be in a secure location before a discussion of what our autopsy and lab researchers found."

Without waiting they start to walk to West Forty-Second Street away from the sealed off thoroughfare.

Awaiting squad car is double parked to take them downtown as the three of them slide in the back seat. The siren is blasting and the vehicle's lights are flashing as the car careens down Broadway to One Police Plaza.

As the vehicle approaches headquarters in front of the building are a multitude of law enforcement cars parked all over the street including many Federal ones.

Johanna hops out of the car and the two of them bypass the security tent making their way to the elevators and upstairs her office. When they open her office door the receptionist informs them she placed the Secretary of Homeland Security in the conference room down the hall with his staff.

The conference room is on the smaller side but contains a great view of uptown from its windows. The Secretary is seated with a few stacks of papers by his side. After the introductions are made everyone is seated, and the Secretary starts speaking.

"Good morning, yesterday a terrorist attack against our country happened in Times Square. From our quick count over one thousand people dies from the attack. The New York Police Department impounded the videos made from private buildings in the area, plus what they made themselves from their traffic light cameras, and are reviewing them nonstop throughout the night. The CDC did some fast analysis of the goat virus which is suspected of killing everyone. This virus is understood to be extinct for over twenty years and is only thought to be found in goats living in the Alborz Mountains of Iran. Somehow it is being mutated and weaponized. The Intelligence Department came up with some thoughts on this, and where someone might be able to obtain the virus?"

"Internationally it could maybe be made by only a few countries. Britain, France, and Germany possess the capabilities to do this kind of thing. Of course, Russia also can do it as well as China. I doubt Iran can, but you never know. They built in secret an advanced facility we are only learning about as we speak. Domestically there is only one facility that even would contain the virus in a safe manner, and it is kept in a dormant state. The laboratory is on Plum Island on the tip of Long Island New York. It is the Animal Disease Center of New York, and it is a federal research facility which studies all kinds of animal diseases. The place is well known in my circle. In the past, they are well assumed to be able to create secret biological weapons during the cold war era with Russia. But their purpose is meant for animals, not humans."

Johanna, sitting in the middle of the table, began to speak.

"Khara I want you to go out there, look around, and find out what you can. I will arrange for a federal search warrant through our office so nobody will give you a hard time. I'll try and finagle for Don Weber to go with you. He is an FBI terrorism expert Mr. Secretary."

The Secretary of Homeland Security chimes in "I'll speak to the FBI and make arrangements for Weber to go with you."

Johanna agreed it would be a helpful addition to the investigation.

"Do you think my partner Detective McMann can be transferred to this case in addition to Don Weber? I worked with Matt McCann for years, and things appear to go without a hitch when he is with me."

"I will arrange the transfer right after this meeting. What you asked for is not a problem" Johanna said.

Khara wanted Matt on this assignment because he covers for her when she goes off police department procedures. Don will not stray and cover for her even if they are engaged. He is too straight, and she knows it.

The meeting is almost over when the Secretary asks a question.

"Johanna, how is the local investigation going on the assassination of presidential candidate Congressman Ferry?"

"We ordered detectives from Manhattan South working on it, but isn't the assassination of a federal case?"

"Yes, it is. I thought I would ask while I am here. The right-wing conservatives in Congress are going nuts with all kinds of conspiracy theories. He is their hero. Now I am on two major cases to solve. Any help you can give me will be appreciated."

"Of course I will Mr. Secretary; besides the detectives, I assigned on the case I will appoint Detective Bennet to co-head the investigation when she gets back from Plum Island in a few days."

"Thanks, Johanna I appreciate your help."
***
When everyone leaves the conference room Johanna calls for Khara to stay behind a minute. They are alone in the room, and Johanna locks the door so they will not be disturbed.

"Tomorrow you will leave for Plum Island at the tip of Suffolk County. Later today I want you to head the investigation into the shooting at City Hall. We are only a few blocks away, and I'll order a squad car to bring you over. Remember I have your back."

"I appreciate everything you do for me Johanna, I won't forget it."

"How about having dinner with me tonight at my condo in Jersey City? After we finish eating we can discuss both cases in bed."

"Sounds good me, I don't need a driver. Please requisition an unmarked car for me to use for the rest of the week."

Johanna grasps Khara's hands and pulls her closer to kiss her. "I missed you Khara."

"I missed you too, and I'll be back by four. Meet you downstairs, and I'll drive to Jersey City with you."

"When you go to the lobby I'll call for one of the motor pool officers to escort you to the garage. You can pick out your own unmarked vehicle."

"Great, thanks see you later."

Both walk out of the conference room and Khara takes the elevator to the lobby while Johanna goes back to her office to make the vehicle arrangements.

When the elevator reaches the ground floor lobby Khara asks the receptionist at the front desk where she can pick up a car the commissioner ordered for her a few moments ago. An officer is called over to escort her to the underground garage where she can be signed out with a vehicle.

While in the elevator to the basement garage the officer asks her a question.

"Detective Bennet, is there any kind of car you would prefer? We maintain four door unmarked sedans as well as some confiscated vehicles from drug dealers down here."

"Let me see the hot cars you confiscated from drug dealers. Years ago I used to be an undercover narcotics officer, and I loved to drive around in their cars once we took them."

"In that case, I might possess the perfect car for you. I'll show you what I am thinking about when we go downstairs."

Once in the garage, they began walking to the rear parking area where the confiscated unmarked cars are stored. As they came closer Khara saw the one she wanted to take out.

"I'll take the Mercedes S 500 AMG in Ruby Black Metallic sitting over there."

"I thought you might like the Mercedes, I intended to show it to you. The car is a hot one. We took it off a major Jamaican drug kingpin in Queens named Hamilton a month ago. Want to try it out?"

"Nope, I drive an M3, and I like them hot and black, like my coffee."

The officer listens and stays silent.

"Nice, now I need you to sign it out in the office before you leave. The keys are inside, I'll ride with you to the front, and we can do the paperwork there."

After she finishes the sign-out sheet Khara gets back in the Mercedes, pulls out of the underground garage, and starts to go a few blocks to City Hall.

Flashing her gold badge to the officer guarding the city hall parking lot entrance she is able to park in front of City Hall.

Khara walks up the stairs and inspects the chipped step the bullet hit after passing through the Congressman.

The podium is inside the main lobby, and dried blood is pooled on the left side of the oak top.

The Secret Service is still on the scene and searching through the park for any clues. One agent walks over to Khara, and before he can say anything she informs him she is assigned to the investigation by the assistant police commissioner on terrorism.

"Did you obtain any clues yet?" Khara said.

"No, but we are waiting for the autopsy to tell us what angle the shot came in from. Once we know we can start using angles, and determine from where the bullet came from. "

"I understand here is my card. Call me and let me know if you come up with anything. I'm going to look around a bit. Thanks, and if I find anything I'll get back to you."

Khara walks out the front doors, down the stairs into the park, and heads for Broadway and Fulton Street without looking back.

As she approaches the building situated on the corner she walks in and takes the elevator to the fourth floor. When the doors open she enters the hallway and continues walking to the end near the stairwell, and the ladies restroom. In a careful and slow way, she opens the door and walks in. Without any hesitation she goes to the last stall she makes sure it is empty and pushes the swinging door open. The latch is pulled shut and the door does not move. Satisfied the epoxy held she takes a medium size hook out of her jacket pocket and ties it to a thin polyester cord. In a slow overhand movement, she tosses it over the top and jerks it up and down until the hook catches the loop on the backpack which is still hanging on the inside of the door. Wrapping it around her forearm so the leather jacket prevents the line from cutting into her skin she starts to lift the backpack upwards until it is even with the upper edge of the door.

With her other hand, she opens the stall door next to the locked one as she loops the line around the inside hook of the open door. Bending her knees she jumps up on the door, swings it around until she can reach over, grab the backpack from the locked stall, and lift it up, over and out.

With the backpack now secured she reaches in, and slides her hand in the backpack feeling the bolt action on the rifle. The weapon is held from the outside with her left hand she releases the slide bolt and withdraws the shell casing putting it in her jacket pocket.

With the backpack in hand, she slips her arms through it, secures it on her back, and walks out of the restroom and down the stairwell to the ground level. In the side lobby of the office building, there is a shipping and print shop with a streetside entrance at the other end of the store. She walks in and asks if they can ship her backpack for her. The clerk is a young girl about eighteen and agrees to box and ship it. After it is it weighed Khara pays in cash and writes out where it is to be sent. The carton is being shipped to her office at the Staten Island precinct. The thought process is if someone should open the box she can say it is evidence and shift the blame to some unknown person. Finished in the shipping store she walks out the street entrance and heads back to her car.

In a matter of minutes, she is in City Hall Park and approaching the Mercedes. She presses the key fob and driver's side door pops open. She sits behind the steering wheel, starts the car, starts to drive out of the parking lot, and heads to the battery where she parks near the Staten Island Ferry in an underground lot.

The water is only a short walk away, and the sun is shining. A boat pulls in and she gets on to take a short ride to Staten Island. Midway through the trip in the harbor she walks outside on the deck and flips the shell casing into the water forever hiding important evidence. Once this is done she sits down back inside and awaits the return trip to Manhattan.

**

It is almost four o'clock, and she is driving up the East River Drive to Police Plaza to pick up Johanna. While on the highway she thinks about being assigned to the assassination investigation. At first, Khara thought it strange but now she realizes this is how Johanna is protecting her. She must assume it is her who shot Ted Ferry, and by assigning Khara to head the team she can redirect the detectives away from the real culprit...herself. In her mind, she thought this is a smart move.

As the Mercedes pulls up to the curb Johanna is walking out of the building, and waves to her. The officers who are assigned to the assistant commissioner say goodnight, and leave when she gets in the car with Khara.

"Hey Khara let's go somewhere for dinner, any suggestions?"

"Feel like a good hand-cut pastrami sandwich? We're not far from Katz's on Houston Street."

"I sure do, it sounds okay to me I miss eating there. It is a long time since I ate at Katz's Delicatessen."

The black Mercedes AMG starts heading north when a red light stops them only a few blocks away from the restaurant. In an instant two thugs who appear to be in their mid-twenties run up to each side of the car yelling at them to leave the vehicle. The one on Khara's side is pointing a gun at her, and ordering both of them to step out of the car.

"Jump out bitches we're taking your wheels."

Johanna unlocks her door and begins to exit. The unarmed thug on her side of the car steps back a foot or two.

"Sit still Johanna, don't move."

With her left hand, Khara presses all the down buttons and the car windows lower at the same time. Now she raises her left arm and waves to them she is getting out of the Mercedes. This conceals a move with her right hand as she reaches in her leather jacket pocket, and withdraws her small snub nose .38 caliber pistol which she always carries with her. With two quick shots through her open driver side window, aimed at the chest of the carjacker with the gun he falls backward on the hard asphalt of the street. His partner, standing near Johanna's door, turns and runs off into the hustle of the street.

"My ears are ringing Khara the shot is loud in here."

"It's better than dead. That's why I rolled the windows down to try to distribute the sound outwards before I fired so the gunshot didn't reverberate too much in here. "

Stepping out of the car she places the snub nose back in her jacket pocket. The shots alerted neighborhood police on foot patrol, and the officers come running to the car. Khara flips her gold badge on a chain out of her blouse for the officers to see, raises her arms in the air so she is not shot by them, and waits for them to approach.

Johanna identifies herself to the officers as a deputy police commissioner, and an ambulance is summoned. Information is given to the responding cops, and she is told television crews are on the way. This incident will be on the evening broadcasts.

The area officer in charge is now on the scene, and lets them go on their way after statements are taken, and the crime scene investigators are present. Johanna doesn't want Khara's identity on the late news since she might be undercover for the investigation. Johanna says she will see Khara fills out a firearms discharge report in her office.

As they drive away Johanna turns to Khara complaining about the noise.

"Khara my ears are still ringing from the gunshots."

"Yes, I know. Give it a week or so, and the sound will go away. Sorry about that."

"I am a little shook up; I never needed to shoot a gun on duty while I am on duty. How can you be so cool under pressure?"

"In case you did not know this about me I thrive on excitement, and this kind of stuff is like a fix to me."

"In that case remind me to send you to rehab soon, let's go eat now because I'm hungry."

Johanna doesn't realize she is sitting in a car with one of the most deadly women in New York City.

Only a few blocks from the restaurant Khara pulls into a parking lot, and they walk to Katz's for dinner. The place is packed, and it is now almost six in the evening. Almost two hours are spent at the carjacking scene until they could leave.

Khara still is wearing her gold badge out of her blouse and hanging on a chain when the young host spots them walking in.

"How many?" he asks.

"Only two how long is the wait?" Khara said.

"Not long I'll find you a table."

They have pushed in ahead of the crowd and seated in the rear. Khara sits facing the entrance as usual when a waiter walks up and asks for their orders.
***

Finished eating Khara pulls out of the parking lot, and heads across town to the Holland Tunnel. Traffic is heavy as it is the height of rush hour, but they are in no hurry to drive to her condo in Jersey City.

Johanna is puzzled about the mass killings.

"I can't believe someone would kill all those innocent people. They must be a terrorist organization, but no one came forward yet and claimed responsibility to this act. Tomorrow when you go out to Plum Island with Don Weber ask them how the virus can be weaponized."

"I plan to ask a lot of questions, don't worry. It will be a thorough investigation."

"Good, also after you left my office today I sent in a request for Detective McMann to go with you to

Plum Island. I'll leave it to you to make the arrangements to meet with him, and the three of you can go together."

"Not a problem Johanna his number is on my cell phone. Detective McMann is very competent. Did any leads come in on Ted Ferry's assassination yet?"

"There is one lead but we are not sure how valid it is. Our intelligence unit received a tip from a Colonel in the Mexican Secret Police who said Ted Ferry is involved with the Ecru Cartel. The suspicion from them is his death is the result of a cartel internecine war about control of the drug trade. When you come back you can join the FBI investigation into his death, but I don't know where it will lead. You might need to end up going to Mexico as a liaison between us and their colonel. You do speak fluent Spanish I understand."

"Yes I lived in the South Bronx as a child, and all my friends spoke the language. I learned to speak Spanish from them." Khara did not tell her she met the colonel the last time she landed in Nuevo Laredo, and he is the drug kingpin now. Some things are better left unsaid.

"Well, it will come in handy. The Holland Tunnel is up ahead and we should be at my place in only a few minutes."

The Mercedes is in New Jersey now and heads for the Turnpike when Johanna's phone rings. It is from the police commissioner and she answers it on the first ring. After a short conversation, she hangs up and tells Khara what he said.

"We discovered a lead on the Times Square attack. One of the video cameras on a building picked up a white van stopping dead center in the middle of Broadway, and a drone is placed on the roof through a top hatch. We are able to obtain the license plate number of the white van through another camera a block away, and Homeland Security is sending the FBI to the registered address as we speak."

"Where are they going?"

"Jersey City, he said he will text me the address. It is registered to a foreign national from the Middle East."

"Okay good, we just arrived in Jersey City. We can head over there now Johanna"

"Khara turn off the next exit and head for the Journal Square. I'll enter the street address into my cell phone map for directions. Give me a moment; it is only a few minutes away. Make a left at the corner and let's go. The commissioner said they obtained a lead on the Times Square terror strike at an address near Journal Square. We are not far from the location."

Because the Mercedes is a confiscated vehicle it is not equipped with a siren or flashing lights. With daring, she drives as fast as she can through intersections which can be treacherous. Not stopping and going through a red light a squad car spots her, and with his lights flashing pulls her over.

In this section of Jersey City, a new big polished black Mercedes AMG with twenty-inch chrome rims is a sign of a major drug dealer, and the officer is taking no chances. The squad car stops behind them and as he approaches places his left hand on the rear trunk lid to leave his fingerprints. This is standard procedure in a traffic stop in case they are needed in the future to prove he did stop them. When he comes up to the side of the large Mercedes AMG his right hand is on the handle of his holstered weapon.

"Nice car you ladies are driving. Please show me your license, insurance, and registration"

Khara rolls down the windows and flashes her badge.

"I am Detective Bennet and this is the New York City Deputy Police Commissioner on Terrorism. We are undercover and need an escort to an address near Journal Square. An FBI operation is going on regarding the Times Square terror attack, and we need to be there fast."

Johanna opens her purse, and also shows her shield to the officer.

"Okay follow me."

He runs back to his car and drives through red lights with Khara following close behind. In a minute or so they are on the street where the operation will be going down.

As they pull up to the house Khara and Johanna exit the Mercedes. They can hear sirens blasting as the FBI tactical and Jersey City swat teams are racing to their location.

The front door to the home with its chipped paint pops open, and a small thin disheveled looking woman with three small children behind her runs out to the stoop. To all appearances, she looks distressed and put together in a sloppy way wearing a kerchief over her head.

Khara dashes in front of the running woman and grabs her arm twisting it behind her back, and begins slamming her to the ground. The officer who escorted them to the address places the woman in handcuffs while Johanna shepherds the three children away from the building. The front door to the building is still open, and masculine voices are heard yelling inside in a foreign language.

Reaching inside her jacket the Sig Sauer is withdrawn from her shoulder holster, the .38 snub nose is in her right hand, and Khara races into the building. Time is of the essence as she does not want to give them a chance to either escape or organize some sort of armed resistance, and does not wait for backup.

The entry hall to the building is narrow with paint peeling off the walls, and the tile floor does not appear to be washed in years. There is an open door to the first-floor apartment, and she runs inside where she notices two men standing in the kitchen who appear stunned she is in there while looking at her, and each holding an AK-47 assault rifle. They stare at Khara with her gold detective's badge dangling around her neck on a chain appears to be in a state of disbelief as to how she is even in there. In an instant, the two men begin to lower their weapons. Not waiting she discharges two shots from each of her guns. In a reflex action, their fingers pull the trigger, and the automatic rifles go off shooting multiple rounds into the ceiling as they themselves fall to the floor.

Sudden silence ensues for a moment until she is aware of more yelling upstairs. Again she cannot make out what is being said, but running through the home she views a wooden staircase by the rear door and starts to run up to the second floor as the timeworn pine steps creak under her weight.

Police cars are arriving and blocking the street to traffic, and ambulances are double parked waiting to be called to action. An armored car arrives and is driven on the block while advancing to the house at the far end of a row of homes.

The FBI agents on the scene are wearing tactical gear with the Jersey City swat team backing them up. The city's bomb squad is also present, and everyone is equipped with a gas mask in case they need one. High above the home, a helicopter is hovering.

From the armored car, a loudspeaker is blaring a warning to the occupants of the home under siege to walk out with their arms raised. The answer to the FBI demand is gunshots being fired out of both second story windows.

The FBI agents usher the handcuffed woman and children down the street. They situate them behind their mobile command center which drove up as the shooting began. The agents waste no time and start to ask her how many more people are in the house.

The woman does not speak to them and remains silent.

With hand gestures, the lead FBI tactical officer communicates to his men. They click the single shot pin off their weapons, and in a single file, a dozen armor clad agents run into the house.

Gunshots can be heard emanating from inside the home. Standing a half block away Johanna spots three figures on the top of the home. She shouts out to the agents standing in front of the home to look up when without warning the men on the roof start to throw hand grenades down to the street. Two parked cars explode when the explosions occur near their gas tanks. The men on top start a fire to the roofs of both adjoining buildings forcing the fire department to rush to the street where they can be easy targets trying to extinguish the fire.

Floating above this crime scene a police helicopter now reports the obvious three men are on the roof throwing grenades down, which everyone is by now aware of, and also sight military weapons laid out on the tar paper next to a small wooden ramshackle shed which used to house pigeons.

The agents inside the home are trapped. They cannot leave for fear of grenades exploding out front; the building is now on fire, and their only way out is through the rear of the home. As a few agents start to leave using the back kitchen door a homemade improvised explosive device in is set off using a cell phone. The device might be connected to one of the men on the roof. The explosion kills many of the agents while the primary kitchen gas line breaks, and natural gas is flooding the room, and home, to a dangerous level.

On the second floor, Khara feels the house shake from the blast and is in a dingy hallway outside a front room where two men are shooting down at the FBI hiding behind cars parked on the street from a window. With no hesitation, Khara empties her .38 into the back of one and a few shots from her .45 stops the shooting at the officers below.

The men start to shoot down at the officers on the street once they run out of hand grenades. Khara releases the empty cartridges from her .38, and using her only quick loader fills the chambers again. Finished she turns and heads back up the staircase to the roof where she sees a few men shooting at the street below. They are yelling something but she cannot understand what it is they are shouting. Taking aim she fires at two men wounding one. They turn and start to return fire. A firefight ensues with multiple shots being sent by both sides.

Using the stairway as cover the open door causes an updraft and Khara now smells the natural gas from the kitchen making its way throughout the house. A few sniffs and she realizes she must scamper off the building in a hurry before the whole place catches fire or collapses.

With a hurried move, she flips her small shoulder strapped pocketbook around and opens it taking out the hand grenade she always carries with her. Pulling the pin she flips the handle off and throws it at them. The short fuse ignites, and the shrapnel ends their resistance.

From the loudspeaker on the armored vehicle, she hears the officer in charge order everyone out of the house. The warning of an imminent gas explosion is being shouted through the loudspeaker.

On the roof, Khara is aware of this warning again, and runs to the adjoining building through a wall of flames, and continues to jump on the next two homes until she throws herself down behind a cinder block firewall on the fourth home's roof, and covers her head with her arms.

Downstairs in the suspect's kitchen, a small fire from the explosion ignites the gas-filled home.

The kitchen gas line explodes, and the home lifts up off the foundation. The wooden frame homes on either side collapse from the underpinning foundation being destabilized. Pieces of debris pierce the homes across the street, and glass windows on many homes shatter from the force of the explosion. The only survivors are the three children and the woman. The FBI agents inside are also killed along with the wounded men on the roof.

Lying flat Khara is shaken when the home she is on begins to shift to one side but does not collapse. When the debris from the explosion stops falling she peers over the firewall and discovers the two homes between her and the exploding home are gone.

Johanna is frantic and searching for Khara through the huge dust cloud. The explosion is immense, and she knows in her heart if she is in the building when it exploded there is no way she will be able to survive.

From the edge of a rooftop at the end of the block, the police below see someone standing alone. The fire department enters the end house and escorts Khara down from the inside.

***

In the mobile command center, the handcuffed woman is brought in for questioning and is sitting on a chair in the center of the trailer with her handcuffs removed.

An FBI intelligence agent sits across from the woman and asks her name. There is no response. A female agent signals for her to stand, she is frisked and patted down. In her pocket, a small wallet is found, but there is no identification in it only a few dollar bills.

Raising her hand she points to her ears and shakes her head from side to side signaling she does not hear. Everyone believes she is deaf.

Two Jersey City policewomen escort her outside, and she is reunited with the children who by now are crying. They will all be taken in for further questioning, and the children placed in protective custody along with the woman. As they are being led away the young woman stops and stares at Khara who in turn gets a good look at the woman's face. The policewomen take them away from the block to a safe location where the FBI will attempt to further interrogate the woman.

Johanna is consulted on what is happening while Khara stands next to her no worse for wear.

Chapter Three

The woman and three children are in police custody as they gather them together at headquarters on Communipaw Avenue for the last time before the FBI leads them away. One small child about seven, in English, asks if she can hug the woman. The handcuffs are again taken off, and the woman is allowed to stoop and put her arms around the young girl. In a quick move, the woman reaches into the small child's side pocket, takes out a pill which she throws in her mouth, and swallows.

"Stop her" someone shouts.

"What happened?"

"She threw something in her mouth and swallowed it."

Mayhem ensues as the police start slapping the unidentified woman on the back hoping whatever she placed in her mouth is still in it and not in her stomach yet. One officer runs over and sticks his fingers deep in her throat trying to make her either spit it out or throw up what she swallowed. An ambulance is called, but it arrives too late. Foam is starting to gurgle out from her lips by the time the EMT's come, and the woman is unresponsive.

The emergency service vehicle rushes her to the hospital where she is declared dead on arrival. Later in the day, her body is taken to the Jersey City morgue for an autopsy.

Khara and Johanna are called in the room after the woman is removed, and the assistant commissioner asks if anyone spoke to the children yet. Nobody answered so Johanna speaks up again.

"Please bring me the oldest child I would like to talk to him."

A thin boy in oversized clothes with bushy hair is brought in, and he is asked to sit on a chair opposite her.

"My name is Johanna, what is your name?"

He shrugs his shoulders and does not answer.

"Do you speak English?"

"Yes, I speak a little. I learn from boys on street."

"What is your mother's name, the one your sister gave the pill?"

"She is not my mother. Her name is Gretchen Popovich. She feeds us when we come here long time ago."

"Do you go to school?"

"No."

"Where is your mother?"

"She died when we come here. Strange men brought us to this home, and Gretchen takes care of us."

"Who are the men in your home?"

"I don't know. They here long time too."

Now sensing a dead end Johanna asks for social services to take the kids away.

"I do not think there is any more we can learn from them. At least we obtained a name to go on. I'll call Homeland Security, and ask them to track her down. Maybe by tomorrow before you leave for Plum Island we can receive an update. Come on Khara let's go to my place and relax a little. It's late now."

The onboard GPS takes them to Caven Point where she parks the Mercedes AMG, and they walk to the elevator to go up to Johanna's condo.

Once inside the apartment, Johanna makes coffee. They sit at her kitchen table discussing the day's events and try to plan for their next move.

"There is not much the NYPD can do with the Jersey City investigation except liaison with their police department. The FBI will in all likelihood take a leading role in this one too. In the meantime I want you to go tomorrow, and inquire if there is anything else you can find out which we might think is useful."

"Sounds good to me Johanna, let's jump in the shower, and after we can go to bed I need to wake up early tomorrow."

***

At five the next morning Khara is again in the shower with her coconut body wash and is ready to start her day. While Johanna is still lying in bed she kisses her goodbye and heads downstairs to the Mercedes.

Last evening before going to sleep she sent a text to Matt and Don to meet her at her apartment by nine in the morning. Now heading to Staten Island, and on to Brooklyn, she is thinking about how the toxin could be spread so fast on Times Square by a drone.

The morning rush hour is starting to be heavy on Staten Island although it is early and still dark outside. This causes the Mercedes to not go over the speed limit but keep up with the traffic flow.

Only a few minutes more and she is able to stop at the yellow valet line in front of her home. With a flip of her wrist, she tosses the key fob to the young man who takes the car and parks it in a private lot a block away.

Once in the apartment she wastes no time and changes her clothes. The top drawer of the dresser is opened; she refills her snub nose and quick loader with .38 caliber bullets. With her right hand grabbing a loaded .45 clip she drops the empty one from her Sig Sauer on to some socks in the middle drawer and slips a new one in her weapon. Bending she slides the bottom drawer open, picks up a hand grenade, and places it in her pocketbook to replace the one she used yesterday.

Now she is ready to leave.

In the hallway, she locks her apartment door and takes the elevator down to the lobby. Next to the concierge desk waiting for her is Matt and Don. After a quick hello the valet brings the Mercedes back to the front of the building, they enter and sit back for a long ride to the end of Long Island.

The trip itself is typical of everyday traffic on the Long Island Expressway East. A lot of cars and trucks are on the highway with each trying to jump ahead of the next vehicle, yet going nowhere fast. Their destination is Orient Point where they need to take a ferry to Plum Island.

Security is high on the island as it is owned by the federal government and the research facility is guarded to keep their deadly work from somehow escaping. The mission of the lab is to safeguard the American food supply by keeping animals healthy. They do this by studying animal viruses and diseases.

The island is self-contained and no unsanctioned foodstuff is allowed to be brought on the premises by individuals, or removed.

Matt is sitting in the rear seat while Don is in the front passenger one next to Khara. While she is driving Don starts a conversation once they leave Queens, and are heading east on the Southern State Parkway.

"Hey, Khara did you give any thought as to when and where you would want us to be married?"

"Yes, there are a few places I can think of I would like to be married. But I am not sure if I can live in the Midwest when you are transferred. It kind of puts a real heavy burden on us getting hitched, you understand what I mean?"

"Yes I do, but it is a good advancement for me. Do you think you can give it some more thought?

Otherwise, I am willing to not take the promotion, and stay in New York with you."

Matt is sitting in the back seat and stays out of the conversation since it does not concern him.

"Listen Don I am happy to be engaged to you, but I feel bad because I know you want this new supervisory position. I cannot see myself living alone in Kansas while you are traveling all over the world for the FBI. I'm a New York City girl... urban... you know what I am saying?"

"I understand. Why don't you speak to Eloise about it? Maybe she'll give you some insight to help make a decision."

"I can't talk to her. She suffered a heart attack and is still in the hospital. I promise I'll talk to her when she is feeling better. But I know you need to tell the FBI soon about your promotion, and transferring to the Midwest. I am sorry but I can't make the commitment you want from me at this moment. I don't know what else to say."

The conversation fell silent after she spoke as the miles rolled on beneath them. At last, they reach Orient Point.

Route 25 becomes Main Road and leaves them by the parking lot at the boat slip to Plum Island. Parked and with the motor turned off they open the doors and stand stretching their legs. The ferry is in front of them as they walk towards it to begin the final leg of their trip.

Although the boat does carry authorized vehicles they leave the Mercedes behind knowing Homeland Security will pick them up at the destination ferry slip on Plum Island, and escort them to the laboratory.

The water is not too rough with a mild wind blowing in off the ocean, and they decide to stay inside the ferry instead of standing on the deck for the quick trip.

In a short time, the boat docks and they can see waiting for them on land a black SUV as they disembark. Both are approaching the vehicle as uniformed security agent is leaning against it smoking a cigarette, and introduces himself asking them to please sit in the vehicle for the ride to the compound's buildings. He starts to explain the island is owned by the federal government, and all biological weapons experimentation stopped years ago. The research lab was to be moved to Manhattan Kansas, and the island sold but a declining real estate market made the sale be postponed until a future time.

"So you are telling us there is no secret weapon experimentation going on in the labs?" Don asked.

The driver answered him and said to his knowledge there is no biological weapons research of any kind on Plum Island at this time. Don decided to press the issue.

"If we want we are able to inspect the actual lab for ourselves, correct?"

"Yes, you will be given a guided tour of the facility. I understand you obtained a federal court order, but you cannot touch anything. Everyone here will need to change into safe suits, and take a sterile shower afterward if you go where the quarantine research is done."

Don expressed interest in going into the lab as he is experienced in biological terrorism while Khara and Matt said they would rather speak to other employees while he is inside the sealed off area. The island is not large, and in a few minutes, they are at the secure research laboratory.

The administrator greeted them in the lobby and is escorted at all times by two armed men who are with him. Don went with the gentleman to the lab while Khara and Matt spilt up with the two guards, and asked to speak to assorted people in the building.

Khara went with her escort, and as they are walking to another building on the grounds she asked if anyone failed to show up for work in the last few days.

"I am not aware of it Detective Bennet, but I don't work in human resources. On the second floor of the main building, we are going now in you will be able to find out your answer. The HR office is up to the staircase you'll see as we walk in. Come with me, and I'll take you to the HR area upstairs."

The entrance to the office is an old half wooden door with opaque glass on the top with a number on it signifying the room.

Khara walks in first and a gray-haired woman is sitting behind a desk with an oversized computer screen on it.

"Good morning I am Detective Khara Bennet from the New York City Police Department. I would like to ask you a few questions if you can spare a moment?"

"Yes of course Detective. You can sit here next to me. What would you like to know?"

"Thanks, are any employees missing from work, or on leave within the last two weeks?"

"None I can think of but let me check my computer."

The woman is typing some queries into the system as she sits back, and waits for the screen to give her an answer.

"Looks like two people are out a lot. One is out about three weeks ago but only gone for four days. The other one is still on vacation and left about the same time but she is not back yet."

"What department did she work in, and what is her name?"

The HR woman hit the F1 key to switch to another screen to find the answer.

"Dr. Gretchen Pupovich worked in the laboratory. She is a biochemical engineer and geneticist and is with us for almost two years. To my understanding, she left to visit relatives in Europe, and did not return yet."

"In my pocket is a federal search warrant, can I please look through her employee file?"

"Sure give me a moment. We store the paper files in the next room."

The woman stands and walks through a small door near her desk, and enters a storage room filled with metal filing cabinets. Khara can hear rollers of the thin tin drawers opening and closing and in a few minutes, the woman returns holding an employee manila folder.

"Here you are. Take your time to look through it."

With the folder in her hands, she sits back in the chair and opens the cover on her lap. The stack of papers is thick as she is turning the pages and looking at each page with care she finds a photocopy of her passport and discovers Dr. Pupovich is a Ukrainian citizen here on a work visa.

"Excuse me, what scientific work is she doing here which an American citizen is not qualified to do?"

"Dr. Pupovich is a world-renowned biochemist who shared a prestigious department chair at a major university in Europe. There are plenty of research positions open to her at top universities in the United States. We are lucky to employ her here and work with us."

"Can you give me a copy of this page please, and I'll leave you alone."

"Not a problem Detective. Give me a minute, and I'll run off a few copies for you."

"Also I would like to speak to the other person who left for four days."

The woman turned to Khara's escort, and told him the individual she wants to talk to is the security guard at Dr. Pupovich's lab and is on duty now."

With her left hand reaching into her back pocket she takes out her phone and calls Matt asking him to go over to question the security guard since he is closer to the laboratory building.

With a handful of passport copies, Khara leaves the office and hastens back to the main building to wait for Matt and Don to return. About thirty minutes later Don walks in with the administrator.

"I asked the lab workers to count the vials of Persian Goat virus and one is different. The one tube contains a colored liquid in it but the color is not the same as the other test tubes. The laboratory manager checked his daily logs, and a Dr. Pupovich is the last person to work with the virus."

"Don we need to leave now and go back. I will talk to you in the car about what I found in human resources."

The three are escorted back to the ferry and soon are in the Mercedes driving on the road to return to Manhattan.

***

Back in the Mercedes speeding along the highway, Khara tells them about Dr. Pupovich.

"She must be the one we are after, but I was present in Jersey City when she committed suicide with a pill. I saw her foam from the mouth and die. We must have reached a dead end. The HR lady said she went to

Europe and didn't return yet. Don you need to call Homeland Security, and check out her goings and comings."

Curious she turns to Matt she asked about the lab's security guard he interviewed.

"I spoke to him, and the man told me he didn't find anything unusual going on in the lab. With no notice, he changed the subject and began to speak about cars. He is a Corvette enthusiast, and told me he bought a new one a few months ago loaded with every option offered."

Both Don and Khara thought it sounded fishy he would change the conversation so fast. Without waiting Don called the HR office on Plum Island and asked for the security guard's home address.

"Okay, he gave it to me. He lives on Fishelton Avenue in Riverhead. It's on our way back so let's stop in, and find out what is going on at his home."

A short drive and the GPS brings them right in front of the house. The street is tree lined with no curbs. The green manicured lawns meet the black asphalt, and a few feet back is a sidewalk giving the area a kind of small-town look, not so suburban; almost a relaxed New England rustic look from the nineteen twenties.

The security guard's house is a typical nondescript single story with dormers in the attic. A driveway is on the side of the home and leads to the backyard where at the end of the pavement is a one car garage.

When they step out of the car they spot one of the garage doors is open enough for a person to slip in the structure. Khara starts to walk down the gravel driveway to the back of the house to investigate. As she approaches the side of the house and almost to the garage automatic gunfire breaks out strafing the

Mercedes from front to rear. Don and Matt rush for cover behind the back of the car and return fire.

Khara grabs her phone and dials 911 to report a code 10-10 shots fired to the operator. She gives the address and identifies herself as a police detective.

With her Sig Sauer in hand, she runs to the rear of the house and kicks in the back door for entry. Multiple shots are still being set off from the front room of the house when Don and Matt decide to stop returning fire. They know Khara can be in the house by now, and don't want to hit her by accident.

Now entering the home's kitchen she hears an automatic weapon still being fired as a trained soldier would use the weapon from the front of the home. Racing through the hallway she comes in behind the shooter.

"Police stop shooting!"

The woman swings her body around aiming at Khara who is standing in the doorway with her gold badge hanging on her chest.

With three quick shots from the Sig Sauer, the woman is hit mid-torso, and is flung backward through the glass of the living room bay window landing on the hedges below adjacent to the house.

Rushing to the broken window to look down at the woman Khara waves to Matt and Don, and calls out to them "all clear, come on in." They scurry through the front door and start to search the home as the Riverhead police arrive on the scene.

Don phones the Plum Island administrator he met today on his phone and explains the situation because he is concerned as to how the woman knew they are coming. Someone in the HR office must be a snitch and told the security guard they are going to stop by his home to investigate him. The HR person must be involved along with the guard because no one else knew where they are headed.

Don orders the administrator to hold both employees until he can arrive back later today to take them in for more questioning, and to call the state police to detain them for further interrogation.

Khara takes out her thin latex gloves from her pocketbook, walks into the master bedroom, and starts to open dresser drawers searching for something, anything, to make sense of what happened a few minutes ago.

On the floor next to the bed is a leather pocketbook. Grabbing the curved leather handle she lifts it up and unzips the top to peer inside. Not being born with patience she flips it over and pour everything out on the bed. Uppermost on a pile of assorted stuff is a Ukrainian passport which she picks up and opens. The picture is of the woman who died minutes ago in the gunfight, and her name is Gretchen Popovich. But she is not the same woman Khara remembers seeing who committed suicide in front of her in Jersey City.

Puzzled she puts the passport in her jacket pocket and walks back to the room where the local police are standing, and waiting for a van to take the body to the morgue for an autopsy.

There is no basement because the home is built on a concrete slab, so Matt goes out back to the garage to find out what is in there. Inside is a brand new red metallic colored Corvette with a white pinstripe swirl on the sides, and a manual transmission. In no hurry he walks around the car and cannot help but observe a large part of the poured concrete floor is broken, pieces removed, and a section of dirt is left instead of cement. Experience tells him the local police need to start digging in the garage to find out who or what is buried down there.

The Riverhead police call in for people and equipment to start breaking up the remaining floor. The police chief is present by now and said he will contact Don with any findings they may discover.

Satisfied there is no longer anything to do in Riverhead they walk back to the Mercedes. Khara, upon approaching the vehicle, finds numerous bullet holes from the front fender to the rear tail lights and notices a fresh pool of liquid something on the asphalt beneath the car.

The Mercedes cannot be driven and needs to be towed back to Police Plaza as some of the multiple shots which hit the car damaged the engine, and it would not turn over when the start button is pressed.

With her mobile phone, she calls for a tow truck and gives the NYPD credit card to the driver. He will take Matt back as a passenger in the truck cab to headquarters with the car.

Once Matt pulls away with the flat-bed truck Khara walks back to the garage, opens the doors all the way, hops in the Corvette, finds the key fob on the dashboard, pushes the start button, and starts to drive out of the building waving to Don to hop in the seat next to her.

"Better buckle up Don."

"Khara what are you doing with this car?"

"I am confiscating it for the NYPD as evidence. The terrorist bitch shot up my wheels, and I need a ride back."

"You are going to turn this over to Homeland Security when you return to the city, right?"

With a sly smile on her lips, she turns her head to face him.

"Of course sweetheart, do you think I'm a car thief?"

After saying this to him she takes the car out of neutral. A powerful car is standing still on the quiet mundane and bucolic street of a sleepy town on Long Island. In a slow and careful manner, she shifts into first and pulls over to the side of the curb and parks for the moment.

Khara starts to set up her phone via Bluetooth to the car's radio so she can play her personal mix. Don sits without saying a word and watching her turn the dials on the dashboard trying to connect her music library to the vehicle. Once connected her right foot smashes the gas pedal to the floor, slams the transmission into first gear, and burns a rubber trail almost thirty feet long down the sleepy block with the rear end fishtailing. Adrenalin is pumping through her veins as she turns the radio volume on high, while it connects with her cellphone. The Rolling Stones are now blasting Jumping Jack Flash from the car's premium speakers as she rockets back to Plum Island as her fiancé holds on for dear life.

***

"Don I don't understand what is going on with this Popovich bitch. First, she dies in Jersey City, and she dies again in Riverhead New York. Something is going on, and it can't be good."

"I feel the same way Khara. Somehow they both are in the country with fake identities. I will report this to the FBI and Homeland Security when I arrive back in my office later tonight. Now we must go back on the ferry to the island and speak to the two suspects being detained."

The Corvette glides into a spot parking in Orient Point, and both of them hasten to catch the ferry to Plum Island seconds before it leaves. As they approach the island the armed escorts are again waiting for them at dockside.

The second time they arrive at the administration building they are ushered into a rear area where the human resources lady is being confined. The administrator informs them she is with two security personnel in a back room. The specific guard they also wanted to be held is now missing, and a search is beginning to look for him.

In no apparent hurry to open the door, Don goes in first and is asked by the woman why she is being detained. He walks over to her, ignores her question, and asks one himself.

"How many years are you been working here?"

"I worked on the island almost ten years."

"Why did you tell the security guard we wanted his home address?"

"I didn't tell him. There is no reason why I would tell him."

Khara steps forward towards the woman and is standing beside her in a menacing stance.

"Listen bitch I know you two are seeing each other so stop with the bullshit, or you are going to prison for treason, and the murder of hundreds of people in Times Square."

"How did you know we are dating? Nobody here knew about it?"

Khara ignored her question and started to drill down on some important information she wanted to know.

"How did Gretchen Pupovich obtain her job here?"

"I am dating the security guard for a while now, and she is my boyfriend's distant cousin from Ukraine. Her credentials are amazing, we needed one more person in the lab, and he said we should hire her. The initial interviews are done in my office, and I found her to be competent on what she is supposed to know to fill the position."

"How long did you date him before your boyfriend suggested her to you?"

"If my memory is correct I would say about two months. In a few weeks from now we are planning to be engaged, why?"

"He set you up. We will delve into his financials, and I am sure there will be a big deposit in his bank account sometime before he started to date you. He needed you to hire her. Once she is in the lab a bonus would more than likely be given to him. The Corvette is to my thinking part of the payoff package he received."

"I feel so used and ashamed. I am sorry, this is terrible."

Don turned to the administrator and told him to keep the woman here until the New York State Police come for her. The FBI will coordinate with the state police, and she will be transferred to federal custody.

Finished in the office they walk outside and ask how the search is going for the security guard. The administrator said the man should be on duty but cannot be found. Yet he feels the suspect did not leave the island as the ferry is the only way to leave. He must still be somewhere on Plum Island.

As the car is brought around to take them back to the ferry a general alarm goes off, and the administrator's mobile phone rings. With his right hand, he withdraws the phone from his pocket and answers it.

"They found the missing security guard. He hid an inflatable boat on one of the beaches on the island, and our small search helicopter spotted him inflating it. They radioed to the patrol cars, and he is cornered on the beach. Come with me, and we'll go right there."

Everyone piles into one of the two four-wheel drive vehicles waiting for them. With lights twirling and sirens blaring they race to the southern side of the island at Pine Point.

As their vehicle approaches the area a helicopter can be seen hovering in the air. They stop next to the other vehicles with flashing lights and hop out racing to the beach.

Three Homeland Security guards drew their guns and are pointing them at the suspect. He is standing in the surf up to his knees holding a test tube in his left hand, and a rope from the inflatable raft in his right one. Nobody is moving.

"If you come any closer I will open this toxic tube, and we will all die. All I want is to leave this island."

Don takes one step forward and introduces himself.

"I am FBI Special Agent Don Weber. Don't make this any harder than it needs to be, let's calm down a bit. I can work with you."

'No stay back. I'm not going to spend the remainder of my life in prison because of this."

"The FBI can cut a deal with you. What is in the backpack you are wearing?"

"I took all the remaining vials of the Persian Goat virus. This bag is worth a billion dollars to the right party. We can all go away, and not work for the rest of our lives. Let me escape, come with me, don't be stupid."

Not aware she is standing behind him aiming her Sig Sauer at the guard Khara is listening to everything Don is saying. The offer of sharing in the money did not enter her mind. The thought which did is should she kill him on the spot or wound him, and be able to interrogate the guard at a later time.

Without taking his eyes off the suspect Don is trying to inch ever closer to the water's edge as he speaks to him in a calm voice.

The man, at last, realizes Don is getting closer and closer and shouts out to him.

"Stay where you are or I will open this vial and kill us all."

Losing patience Khara aims for the guard's mid-chest where his heart would be and lowers her aim to his left knee. Two shots ring out, and he collapses in great pain into the breaking waves with Don racing into the water grabbing his wrist as the waves come crashing down on the pair.

The other Homeland Security officers rush into the surf after Don and help drag both of them onto the beach. Don is still holding the forearm of the suspect with the deadly vial clutched in his hand.

The security guard is lying on the beach crying out in pain while curled up in a fetal position.

An ambulance is on the way to bring him to a hospital on the mainland with the security officers accompanying him. Don looks at Khara and smiles.

"I'm glad you didn't kill him. The FBI can try to find out what information he might be harboring about the terrorists. After the transport takes him to the emergency room I will go with the Homeland Security officers until I am relieved. You head back to the city, and I'll speak to you later."

Before she is escorted back to the ferry Don asks Khara how she knew the human resources lady is dating the security guard, and why she took the chance of kneecapping the guy in the water. "What if he opened the vial in the surf, and we all would be dead by now?"

"The first time I went to see her about any employees either missing or absent she asked me to sit in a chair next to her which is behind the desk. I remember seeing her in a photograph in a nice bright chrome frame near the computer screen. The stupid bitch is standing next to a brand new red Corvette with the same custom white swirl on its side as the one we found in his garage. I made an intelligent leap of faith she is dating him. Otherwise, why is a photograph of someone else's car on your desk? There is no other rational reason. It is the only explanation I can think of for the picture being on her desk. And as to why I chanced shooting him in the knee, and not in the chest the answer is easy. If I killed him you wouldn't be able to speak to him later about what he knew, or why he did what he did. The reason I kneecapped him is I assumed he would fall in the surf in tremendous agony, and give you an opportunity to grab his wrist before he could open the vial. I figured the pain would be too intense for him to do anything except collapse into the water which would act as a cushion to the test tube if he dropped it preventing the glass from breaking. I took a chance and it paid off. I'll see you back in Manhattan, bye."

Chapter Four

The red Corvette screeches to a stop in front of Khara's apartment house in Brighton Beach. Parked at the yellow valet line she flips the key fob to the young man running to the car who waits under the entrance awning for cars to arrive.

"Nice new car you're driving Ms. Bennet?"

"Not mine it is a friend's I'm using for a while."

"Still nice wheels, I'll put it in the lot for you."

"Thanks, and drive carefully. It's brand new."

Tired from the day's long hours she walks through her building's entrance and presses the button to take the elevator up to her floor.

The concierge lifts his head up from reading at his desk when she enters the lobby, and dashes around from the marble counter to speak to her before she goes on the elevator.

"Excuse me Ms. Bennet, but Olga asked me to tell you she would like to talk to you as soon as you come in today."

From her previous experience she is aware this must be for something important. In the past when her dead boyfriend Al used to call her it is always for something urgent, not a normal how is your day going conversation. With Al killed on the orders of the Mexican Secret Police Colonel it now appears Olga is going to call the shots together with her lover Viktor, and the Russian mob in the United States.

The elevator takes her up to the penthouse where she is greeted by two Russian Special Forces bodyguards standing outside an apartment door made of solid steel. One of the men uses his mobile phone to announce Khara is on the floor waiting by the front door, and in a few seconds, Olga herself opens it.

"You are in time for dinner Khara, come in. I ordered platters of corn beef and pastrami from the kosher delicatessen you took us to right down the avenue. Also, your favorite Dr. Browns Black Cherry soda is here. Junior is joining us for dinner tonight because we are going to engage in a serious discussion during dinner concerning certain matters."

Still wearing her leather jacket, and armed to the teeth she walks behind Olga and sits in the middle of the dining table opposite Junior.

"It's always a pleasure to meet you again Khara."

"Thanks, Junior, same here."

Khara is looking past him when she spots Big Boy sitting on two seats of a sofa on the other side of the living room.

"Hey Biggie, how're you doing?"

Big Boy answers her with a huge thumbs up signal.

Viktor takes control of the meeting as the platters of food is passed around the table.

"Our international network informed me the Colonel wants to control not only the exporting of his drugs to this country but other countries as well. This means he needs to be rid of us, and Junior. We cannot let this happen."

Khara sits back and listens. Not stupid she is reading between the lines and realizes someone is going to need to go finish off the Colonel, and since she speaks fluent Spanish the job will in all likelihood fall to her to do.

Junior puts his sandwich down, and gazes across the table right at Khara, as does Olga and Viktor. With everyone's eyes staring at her Khara decides it is time to speak to them with total honesty.

"To be upfront with you I can help you out, no problem, but at the moment I am on two cases, and might not be able to travel right away. The most important case is the Times Square terrorism one, and the second case is the assassination of Congressman Ted Ferry."

In a strong Russian accent, Viktor starts to speak to her concerns.

"Tell me what you need help with regarding the terrorism case. I possess contacts in the intelligence field in many European countries, and we may be able to help you out."

"I came across a lead on a biological geneticist from Ukraine by the name of Dr. Gretchen Pupovich. I think there is something not right about her. Today alone I saw her commit suicide in Jersey City, and later I killed another woman by the same name near Plum Island New York. How many Pupovich's are in this country with the same passport? I kill one and another pops up. One Pupovich dies and refuses to stay dead. I don't know why I am meeting so many dead women with the same unusual name here?"

"Let me contact my sources tonight, and by tomorrow sometime I should be able to obtain some information for you. For the past month, my men are tracking the Colonel watching his movements and schedule. When the timing is right I will send you and Olga to Mexico to resolve our problem with him. Meantime let's eat."

Everyone at the table knew about the assassination case. It is Viktor who obtained the weapon for Al, Junior's father, to send to Khara in Virginia with Big Boy. This is a case they solved themselves because they caused it to happen. Their concern, it appears to Khara, is with the drug money they will be losing if the colonel is not taken out. Also, the possibility exists they all could be killed just like Al, including her, and she understands nobody at the table wants to be shot in the head.

Finished eating she says her goodbyes and leaves the penthouse after dinner. Khara takes the elevator down to the fourth floor and enters her apartment. After opening the door she glances up and takes note of a small LED light set back into the ceiling over the inner doorway. Nobody is aware an electric eye is installed by the entry hall, and if the red LED light goes on she recognizes someone tripped the circuit and is in her apartment waiting for her. After Al surprised her once when she came home to find him in her bed she contracted with a local security firm to install this setup. Double locking the deadbolts on the door she puts her weapons down on the kitchen counter and goes into the bedroom to be ready for the night.

After a relaxing warm shower using her coconut body wash she gets in bed and starts to think about her schedule for tomorrow. There is Don to contact to see what he found out from the wounded security guard, and she needs to call Johanna to check in with her, and finally, she remembers she sent a UPS package to the precinct in Staten Island addressed to herself.

With the remote in her hand, she flips on the television and falls asleep to the droning white noise of the late evening news shows.

***

At six the next morning her alarm goes off at the same time Johanna is calling her on her phone.

"Hey, Khara how did you make out yesterday on Plum Island? I am told a few officers from the area, plus you three are involved in a shooting in Riverhead."

"Yes, I guess you read the police reports from the state police. It is a pure self-defense shooting, and also in the report should be two witnesses. I also loaned a Corvette from the shooter."

"I read all about it. We'll deal with the car later. I need a report on the women. Homeland Security is in on this also, and they don't understand how two women with the same passport can be in this country. The Secretary is tightening the screws because he doesn't want Congress to find out about this development and make it into a political football."

"It is understandable. Last night I met with some sources I use for international matters, and they are researching the double identification thing with their European informants. I am told depending on what they find out I might need to go to Europe. Will the department send me there because they will only deal with me?"

"Let me know when they come up with something and I'll take care of sending you. I don't foresee any problems concerning a trip for you. I'll contact Homeland Security today and find out if we can coordinate sending you to investigate."

"Great, I must go to Staten Island today and report into my precinct. I'll catch up with you later, bye."

Alone in her apartment, she walks to the bathroom and turns on the shower when her phone rings again. With a quick glance, the caller ID tells her it is her fiancé Don.

"Good Morning Don, what time did you arrive home yesterday?"

"I arrived home late because I needed to go back to the office and file my report while the facts are still fresh in my mind. How did the rest of your day go?"

"I think as well as can be expected, I guess. As soon as I arrived home I ate dinner with Olga and Viktor, and we discussed a bunch of things. This morning I spoke to Johanna and I might be sent to Europe on this case."

The thought of mentioning Junior never entered her mind so Don is not aware an organized crime boss also ate dinner with his fiancé.

"Do you want me to find out if I can go along if you go there? My specialty is terrorism you do remember?"

There is no way she wants Don to go with her. If Olga decides to go it is a huge plus as she speaks fluent Russian and some Slavic languages too. With the knowledge of her being a deadly assassin, Khara thinks Olga would not take kindly if he came along, and might also kill him if he hampered her work ever so little. How would she explain his death to Johanna she thought to herself?

"No Don I want you to stay here. I need a confidential source in the states if I do go. There is not a lot of time and I must run, my shower is on, and I want to check into my precinct this morning. Talk to you later, bye."

When the water is warm enough she hops in the shower grabbing her coconut body wash and is in and out in no time. After drying off she takes her Chanel No.5 off the cabinet shelf, and the par-fume is sprayed all over her body.

Before she gets dressed she walks into her bedroom, opens a dresser drawer, and reloads the spent clips from her Sig Sauer, also replacing the .38's she shot in her quick loader. Now opening the bottom drawer to her dresser she takes out a ten-second fused grenade and places it in her pocketbook. Satisfied with her weaponry and feeling confident she is ready to dress. The clothes closet door is swung open, and Khara starts to take out her clothes for the day.

Ready to leave she calls downstairs to the concierge to bring her M3 around to the valet stand. On the way out she places her throwing knife in her right boot sheaf and leaves her apartment.

Her sense of peace is somewhat lost with the knowledge the Colonel wants to kill everyone associated with Olga, Viktor, and Junior.

Khara scrutinizes the area to be certain she is not being watched as she is standing still on the sidewalk by the painted yellow valet line on the curb. People are passing by her going to the train station or the bus stop along with the morning rush hour traffic which is not unusual.

The M3 is coming around the corner and turns onto her street, and the valet stops the car in front of where she is standing. Khara thanks the valet and sits in the car, buckles up, and shifts into first gear heading for the Verrazano Bridge.

The BMW M3 is driving on the Belt Parkway and passing Gravesend Avenue when she opens her moonroof since it is a bright sunny morning, and not too cold. She is trying to calm her nerves which are on hyperdrive, her senses are alert, and she finds it hard to ease up. Experienced in dealing with the Ecru Cartel she is cognizant they will not stop until either she is killed or they are all killed. One of them will survive, not both, and Khara is well aware of the danger.

With a flip of a finger, the radio is turned on, and her personal mix is picked up from her mobile phone. The speakers are blasting "That Old Time Rock and Roll" as she shifts into third gear with the engine whining as it is approaching the red line rpm on the tachometer.

Her nerves are starting to unwind a bit as she drifts into a focused driving mode not paying attention to the cars coming up behind or on her sides. A robotic mindset is driving her to the bridge as she starts to daydream about seeing Eloise again in the hospital. Fort Hamilton's chain link fence is high on the right of a short hill as the M3 is passing by, and Khara is calm and collected.

The car in front of her stops short with its rear lights glaring red, and waking her from an almost catatonic state. With cat-like reflexes, she slams on the brakes and avoid rear-ending the car which stopped in front without warning. With a lot of luck, the M3 is in the right lane, and she turns a few feet off the road onto the grass from the asphalt to avoid a collision.

The sudden stop causes her to shift forward in her seat as she recognizes the sound of a gunshot ring out from a rusted blue car with a roaring exhaust problem to her left. The bullet whizzes by the back of her head piercing the driver and passenger side windows of her new BMW.

From the car's quick halt in movement, her head jerked forward and almost slams into the center of the steering wheel. The seatbelt tightens its grip on her and prevents this from happening. Out of the corner of her eye, she can see the flash from the gun barrel, and again the bullet misses her as she thinks due to their probable lack of marksmanship training.

With her right hand, she reaches inside her jacket and withdraws her Sig Sauer to return fire. All traffic jams unwind at some point and this one does too as traffic lets up, and the shooter's car speeds away in the middle lane.

Pinned in she cannot turn into the middle lane to follow them due to oncoming traffic, and there are cars in front and behind; in frustration, she yells out to herself.

"Screw this shit you bastards. You're not going to run away from me."

Pissed at what happened she shifts into second gear as she turns to the right, flips on her police lights in the grill and siren, and smashes the gas pedal to the floor. The M3 starts to drive on the grass at a sharp angle heading for the entrance to the bridge's ramp bypassing traffic stopped in the right lane. Khara is hoping to cut them off before they go on the bridge.

The BMW M3 is designed to be a sports sedan with a powerful engine and superb cornering abilities. The problem Khara is experiencing is this car is not meant for off-road driving. The almost thirty-five degree sloping uphill grass beneath the fort's fencing is rough and bumpy as the M3 speeds towards the cars turning on the bridge.

A small gap opens as the cars make the curved turn upwards on the ramp, and she aims for the spot cutting off a car in the line.

About eight car lengths ahead she spots the blue car entering the turn to go on the bridge. The M3 is too far back to discover if it goes on the top roadway or the lower one. The top of the bridge entry ramp splits, and she needs to make a decision on which one to take, the lower or upper levels of the bridge.

A decision to turn is made and she takes the upper roadway because when it empties on the toll plaza she will be able to look down, and either spot the blue car come out from below or approach the toll booths from the higher road she is on, and speeding ahead of the M3.

In a sharp jerk, she yanks out a chain from under her blouse which holds a gold detectives badge, and is bouncing on her chest as she downshifts to second, and turns the steering wheel careening around the slower cars ahead of her changing lanes with wild abandon.

There are at least eight cars lined up in front of each toll booth. The blue car is fifth on one of the toll lines.

In an effort to catch the gunmen she is speeding on the bridge toward the toll booths when the M3 slips between two lines of cars, and stops twenty feet in front of the concrete toll booth barrier. With the Sig Sauer in hand, she jumps out of her car and runs back towards the blue car. The passenger in the car turns his head and spots her coming after them, and leans out the window starting to shoot at Khara.

With a few quick pulls on her trigger, the Sig Sauer spews out its deadly fire. The gun is aimed at the car's front window poking holes through the glass and penetrating the interior of the vehicle. The passenger who is shooting at her is struck multiple times and drops his weapon out of the window landing on the plaza concrete.

The driver jumps out his door and stands behind it using the car as a shield while raising a sawed-off pump action shotgun.

Khara, standing in the middle of a cauldron of noise, perceives the unique sound of a pump action shotgun being loaded. Keesh keesh the action bar is pushed and pulled back now ready to fire. Khara falls to the ground as the driver pumps off shot after shot hitting cars all around where she fell to avoid being hit. Innocent drivers sitting in their cars near her waiting to pay the toll are hit, windows shatter, and car horns are starting to blow merging their sounds with her M3's siren which she did not turn off.

To avoid the shotgun blasts she is rolling on the ground towards the blue car as this prevents her from being targeted, and the police from seeing her. Near the car, she is able to look at his ankles on the other side of the vehicle and aims for them. The shooter begins to run around the front of his car looking for her when Khara fires multiple times, and he drops to the ground. The gunman's right foot is shot out from under him as his ankle is smashed from her bullets.

The police hear the M3's siren, multiple car horns, also a lot of gunshots, and they come running in mass toward the gunman. They are willing to engage him in a firefight.

Although he is writhing on the ground in pain the shooter is still holding his weapon when he turns his head under the car and spots Khara. The assassin is lying on the concrete plaza when he turns over on his belly, raises the shotgun to his chest, and starts to aim under the car at her. For protection, she is using the blue car's tire as a shield as he is able to fire off one blast. He rolls over on his back to reload, and again she can hear the unique sound of keesh keesh. With care, she peeks around the tire as the Sig Sauer spits out shot after shot towards him blasting him in the upper body and head with blood and brain matter spraying all over the toll plaza floor.

Not wanting to be shot by the approaching transit police Khara slips the Sig Sauer back into her shoulder holster, raises her arms high above her head and remains sitting with her back leaning against the tire of the blue car awaiting the police to approach her.

With untypical patience, Khara sits still and wants them to be able to see the gold detective badge on her neck chain so she is watching out for the officers to discover her.

After showing her identification the area is cordoned off when she inspects the blue car reaching in to turn off the vehicle. With the ignition key in hand, she places it in her left jacket pocket. The transit police start to search the car for any clues to the two body's identification going through the trunk and glove box.

Khara walks around to the front of the vehicle. The sticker on the bullet-ridden windshield tells her this is a rental car from Texas.

The realization by Khara the Colonel is now going after anyone associated with Olga or Junior is driven home to her. From experience dealing with the Cartel, she realizes full well this is only the beginning, there is only one way to end it. The Colonel needs to die before she does.

***

After all the damaged cars are towed away, ambulances gone, and the bodies taken to the morgue Khara turns around driving her windowless M3 back to Brooklyn. The valet at her apartment house takes the BMW to the buildings secured parking lot and brings out the red Corvette for her.

The time is midafternoon, she still is behind schedule, and not able to report into her Staten Island precinct. Khara will try again as she slips behind the steering wheel, shifts into first gear, and heads out towards the bridge.

With no interference, this time the Corvette reaches the precinct without incident. She parks in front of the stationhouse and walks in waving to the desk sergeant. The rear wooden staircase leads up to the area where the detective squad is located. Matt is in his cubicle and calls out to her as she passes by.

"The radio reported on your activities on the way in this morning Khara."

"I'm not surprised. Did my package come for me yet?"

"Yes, I placed the box next to your desk."

"Okay, thanks, Matt I appreciate it."

"I'm curious, what's in the box Khara?"

"Believe me you do not want to know. Let's leave it at that."

Turning into her secluded work area she now opens the box, lifts out the backpack, and slips it in the kneehole of the desk to be secured and out of sight. With her foot, she makes sure it is all the way under.

The precinct captain is told she is in the building and calls up to her to please see him in his office. Not wasting any time she stands and pushes her chair all the way in under the des. Starting to go downstairs to her commanding officer's office she walks past Matt's area as he is also coming out at the same time, and they meet in the walkway.

Both discover the captain requested they come to his office together so they knock on his door, and he calls out to them to enter.

"Both of you sit down. I would like to say it is a pleasure for both of you to work here under my command, but the headaches from one of you are way too much to bear. So I am pleased to inform you the Deputy Commissioner on Terrorism is transferring both of you to One Police Plaza to work in her department. Good luck, and clean out your personal items. Tomorrow you report to headquarters."

As they leave the office Matt is puzzled.

"I didn't expect this Khara. I know you said you would ask for me to be transferred with you, and I went to Plum Island, but you never said it is happening now."

"I told you I mentioned it to Johanna, and she said she would take care of it, but she didn't say as to when. My guess is she liked my suggestion. In any case, we're back in Manhattan again Matt."

"Looks this way, let's grab our stuff, and I'll meet you tomorrow at Johanna's office."

"Sounds good to me, I'll see you then."

Khara goes back to her desk, reaches under, and grabs the backpack, empties her locker of a few beauty necessities kept in it, and is ready to leave. There are no personal items she keeps on her desk or in the precinct. The truth is she is not at all sentimental and does not own any keepsakes to speak of.

Once she fires up the Corvette's engine in front of the precinct her phone rings, it is Johanna. When Khara took the car from the garage it went so fast there is not enough time for her to set up the connection between her phone and the Corvette's hands-free phone system. With her legs pressing down on the floorboards she scooches up in the driver's seat, and she slips her phone out of her pocket to answer the incoming call.

"Hey, Johanna what's up?"

"Meet me at my place in an hour. I'm on my way home and I want to speak to you about the Times Square killings. I obtained some information, and I need to speak in private."

"I'll be there in twenty-five minutes or so; I'm in Staten Island now. I will be there soon."

The car pulls out of the parking spot, and in minutes she is on the back 440 highway to the Bayonne Bridge. Once in New Jersey, she is heading to Caven Point where they are to meet as the Corvette is going way over the posted speed limit.

The ferry is pulling into the slip from Manhattan with Johanna as Khara parks and walks towards the pier. The breeze from the bay is strong, and a little chilling as the white caps break below where she is heading.

Johanna bounds off the rocking boat onto the floating ramp to the pier greets her with a quick kiss, and they walk back to her condo holding hands.

Once inside the apartment, the coffee maker is started, and they sit at the kitchen table with their hot cup of brown caffeine to warm up. Johanna is sitting opposite her and begins to speak.

"I heard about the shooting today by the toll booths at the Verrazano Bridge. Four innocent drivers are shot, and one died at the scene. We can't find out anything about these men except the car is a rental from Laredo Texas. Homeland Security is waiting for a fingerprint check to come back. What do you know about them, if anything, since you are involved and they are intent on hunting you down?"

"The vehicle plates are from Texas, and the sticker on the windshield is from a Laredo car rental agency. My educated guess is they are from the Mexican Secret Police, and the remnants of the Ecru Cartel like the Homeland Secretary mentioned to us."

"You are probably right so I may let the FBI handle them for us."

What Johanna did not know is Khara is not going to wait if given the choice.

"Is this what you needed to speak to me about tonight Johanna?"

"No, but I wanted to find out your thoughts on another subject. What I wanted to tell you is the FBI inspected the passports of the two Gretchen Pupovich women, and they are forgeries. The women did not come into the country with those passports. The FBI told me according to their experts the paper on the passports are printed on is not American made paper. They are close, and look good, but are fake passports. Only a foreign country would be able to obtain the resources to print them. Are there any ideas you can think of about this matter Khara?"

"No, but my landlords are from Russia. I spoke to them yesterday, and they said today they might be able to secure an answer from their sources as to who Popovich is."

"Khara be careful dealing with them. My department maintains a large dossier on both of them.

They are former KGB agents. Viktor, according to the CIA before he retired he is one of their top people, and he emigrated and settled in Brooklyn with his girlfriend. How well do you know them?"

"On different occasions, I see them in the elevator, and I say hello. Sometimes we talk about different things, nothing much really. Yesterday I saw both of them and asked if they could reach back to their sources for me about Popovich."

"Let me know what they discover about her. Also don't become too close to them. They are on the FBI watch list as leaders of a Russian organized crime syndicate."

Although she shouldn't be surprised at Johanna knowing about Olga and Viktor she is taken back the FBI is keeping track of them. The thought is now crossing Khara's mind is Johanna using her as a pawn in a national security game. The question is Don, her fiancé, using her also to be close so he can keep track of her landlords. In the past, he stayed at her place many times, and is he there to plant a secret recording device, or did he stay with her because in his heart he wanted to be with her?

Self-focusing on her inner thoughts she missed what Johanna said to her.

"Khara I asked you a question?"

"Sorry my mind started to think about the cases, and I missed what you said."

"The question is what time today are they supposed to be back to you with their information. If we can use them to track the real Popovich we might be able to use the knowledge down the road to deport both of them, or charge them with terrorism."

"They didn't give me a time. I'll go home after the coffee is finished and try to speak to them."

"How about staying for dinner, and I'll order in some food. After we eat maybe we can relax a bit before you go, what do you say?"

"Sounds good; order from the Italian restaurant all the way uptown on Avenue C in Bayonne. I like their food."

***

Early the next morning Khara is in the Corvette going through the Holland Tunnel on her way home. In her mind, she is trying to piece together the puzzle of how everything is going to play out. If only Eloise would be out of the hospital already she thinks to herself. In the past when she speaks to her things, to her way of thinking, are in focus a little better. As the car leaves the tunnel and enters the curved roadway in Manhattan she turns off to go uptown. "Screw it," she thinks to herself. "I'm going to speak to Eloise because I need to talk to her now."

The drive uptown is not too bad, but the crosstown traffic is heavy as rush hour is starting.

The parking garage is beginning to fill up as families come to visit their loved ones in the hospital. Khara arrives with others who are looking to park. She drives in the underground garage, leaves the Corvette, and takes her parking lot ticket with her as she walks to the hospital's main entrance.

With her badge out of her blouse flashing her gold shield to the security guard she is admitted inside and takes the elevator upstairs to ICU.

The head nurse on duty informs her Eloise late last night transferred out of ICU, and Khara heads for the room determined to clear her mind. It is not hard to find the room, and when entering finds Eloise is sitting up in bed eating her breakfast.

Eloise looks up from a plate of runny scrambled eggs and toast, and she places her fork down as Khara enters the room.

"Khara what a pleasant surprise, come kiss me hello, and sit down on the bed right next to me."

In measured steps, she walks to the hospital bed, and as she bends to kiss her on the lips Eloise places her right hand behind Khara's head pulling it in towards her face, and holding Khara in a long loving kiss.

The other bed in the room is empty at the moment when Khara realizes she is in a semi-private room, and so she believes she can speak to Eloise in confidence.

"I am overjoyed you came to sit with me when the hospital first admitted me to ICU. What is going on with you?"

"Not much, I am busy at work."

"This morning when I woke up I am able to turn on the news, and it appears to me the whole world is exploding right here in New York. Did you involve yourself in any part of what is going on?"

"Depends on what part of the explosion you are speaking about."

"Well I know you wouldn't kill all those innocent people in Times Square on a whim. Are you involved in any part of it?"

"Yes, I am. Johanna wants me to speak to my Russian landlords, and find out any information they might be able to obtain from their old KGB sources."

"It makes sense Khara. She is trying to cover all the bases. A Terrorist committed a terrible crime killing many people in our country. And can I assume you are somehow involved in the presidential candidate being killed."

A sly smile crossed Khara's face, and she does not reply to the question about Ted Ferry being shot.

"I am on the Times Square case working under Johanna's direction. Also, I am heading up the city's investigation of the assassination. There is a strong chance I might need to travel to Europe to flesh out the information gathered so far. Also, the Colonel from the Mexican Secret Police wants to eliminate his two partners in the country, Olga, and Junior. Somehow they know I am involved with them, and he tried to kill me yesterday at the Verrazano toll plaza. The thing is, as you can see I survived, and they didn't."

Eloise is holding Khara's hand in hers and asks in a low voice, almost a whisper "is there anything you would like to speak to me about in total confidence?"

Khara moves closer on the bed and explains her thoughts and misgivings about Johanna and Don. Self-preservation is foremost on her mind at the moment. As a clinically diagnosed psychopath, she possesses no real emotions towards either of them, yet they fill a void in her life at some level of physical need.

Her back resting against a pillow Eloise starts to tell Khara to "go with Olga to Europe if possible, not Don. She will cover your back plus she speaks many languages, and you only speak Spanish. Don Weber will turn you in if he thinks you are involved with the presidential shooting; so give yourself some space from him for a while till the investigation cools down a bit. Go to Europe. I'll speak to you when I am out of here. Maybe we can go on another cruise to Bermuda together?"

"Yes, I would love to go on a cruise with you when I come back from Europe."

"Okay Khara I'll make all the arrangements. Of course, I will pay the expenses again as before. Come and kiss me goodbye before you leave."

Satisfied with her counsel Khara kisses her, and walks back to the parking garage, reclaims the Corvette, and drives to Brooklyn to speak to Olga and Viktor.

Chapter Five

There is, to her, a calming effect in the salty sea air as she inhales the soft breeze wafting in from the Atlantic Ocean as she stands on the sidewalk by her building. The nervous energy she struggles to control is rumbling in her gut with the knowledge challenges will soon come into her life. The doorman greets her with a friendly smile while opening the etched glass doors for her to enter.

In the lobby, the concierge, situated behind the marble desk reading a Russian newspaper, informs her Viktor and Olga would like her to come to their penthouse apartment as soon as she arrives in the building. The two heavily armed Russian men sitting on the sofa across from the elevators wave hello, and smile at her. There are no catcalls or rude comments made toward her. Everyone of Olga's men respects her with the common knowledge Khara is as dangerous as Olga.

The soft violin music playing in the elevator unnerves her as her Adrenalin is starting to bubble up in anticipation of the information Olga and Viktor will in all likelihood tell her when she reaches the penthouse floor.

The elevator door opens on the penthouse floor, and Khara enters a small lobby with another Russian guard sitting behind a small table reading. The husky man guarding the penthouse is aware of who is on the way up due to his earpiece, and he appears relaxed with his weapon still holstered on his hip.

A quick knock on the door, the solid steel opens rather slowly, and Olga greets her with a serious expression on her face. Viktor is sitting in his lounge chair waiting for her to enter.

"Come in Khara I wanted to tell you we received some information about Gretchen Popovich from our sources in Moscow."

Khara realizes this cannot be news she might want to hear because Olga is not smiling.

"Through our FSB contacts we found out the woman you are looking for is the leader of a Chechen rebel group near Grozny. The revolutionaries may want to use whatever they sprayed in Times Square for their cause, but no one is sure. The Russian Army is looking for her, and they placed a large bounty on bringing her in dead or alive."

"So I guess this means I need to go find her somewhere in Chechnya. What does she look like?"

"The FSB contacts we are in touch with informing us she is about five foot six and one hundred twenty pounds or so with short black hair and sky blue eyes. There is nobody who can find pictures of her only this description they obtained from a double agent working in the rebel group."

"At least I received something to work on when I go to Chechnya."

"Not by yourself Khara. The FSB wants me to come back to try to find and kill her. Although they asked me I understand what they want is more than a request. Viktor and I feel this is our payback for the favors they do for us. How soon can you be ready to fly?"

"Let me go downstairs to call the Deputy Commissioner and obtain her permission. Otherwise, I'll take vacation time off."

"Okay let me know because I must begin to pack a few things myself."

Viktor tells her to ask for a diplomatic passport for Olga and herself. This way if they are in trouble the CIA can request each be returned. Without those passports, they could end up in a Russian prison, or worse if things go wrong.

Khara understands what he said, leaves and enters their lobby to take the elevator down to her floor, nodding goodbye to the security guard still sitting in his chair.

The apartment door opens, she goes in, lifts her chin up, and glances at the alarm light she installed. The small LED light is green so she enters, and without wasting anytime calls Johanna.

"Hey, Johanna are you in your office yet?"

"Yes, what did you find out?"

"This is a big international operation. Homeland Security needs to make diplomatic passports for Olga and me. We need to fly to Europe to find the real Popovich."

"I'll call the Homeland Secretary now in Washington and make the arrangements. I want to confirm her name with you according to the FBI files I am given on her. The information spells her name Olga L_e_v_o_v_n_a L_e_i_n_s_k_i, correct?"

"No, she spells her name with a Y. She spells it L e v I n s k y."

"Olga is Jewish?"

"I can't answer your question because I never asked her. There is a chance someday I might ask."

"Not important. I need a day for the passports to be made and sent up here by personal carrier from Washington. Meanwhile, you can continue to work on the assassination of Congressman Ted Ferry."

"Okay, later today I'll be in the city to follow up on the investigation. By the way, where did they tow the blue sedan which was involved in my shootout at the bridge?"

"The car is parked at your old precinct's secured lot in Staten Island. The central evidence one is full so the crime lab will be going to the one in the back today about noon to go over the vehicle. After they are finished the department will need to tow the car to a Brooklyn yard after they are done searching for clues."

"I'm going to revisit the car for clues before I drive into Manhattan."

"Fine Khara I'll talk to you later."

Once Johanna spelled out Olga's name Khara instantly knew she is not being told everything; the building where she lives and the Russian mob is being carefully watched by our national law enforcement services.

Khara hangs up, puts her backpack on the kitchen counter, and takes out the sniper rifle. The latex gloves are slipped on her hands as she starts to disassemble the weapon rubbing down all the parts trying to erase her fingerprints. After she is finished the gun is placed back in the bag and zippered shut.

Before leaving her apartment she showers spritzes on her Chanel No.5, puts fresh latex gloves in her pocketbook, and changes her clothes. Now the day can begin on a positive first step.

When the elevator door opens she walks out of the lift and enters the marble-tiled lobby of her building when the concierge tells her Viktor is arranging for her M3 windows to be repaired. With a wave of his hand, one of the valets runs out the back door to bring the Corvette around so she can leave.

The doorman opens the massive front door for her, and as she is approaching the red sports car she takes the backpack off and places the bag behind the driver's seat in the rear trunk area. With her right leg in the sports car already she slips down into the seat and smells the new leather interior, turns the car on, hears the powerful engine purring in neutral, shifts into first gear, and heads for Staten Island to her old precinct.

The parking spaces at the front of the precinct are full when she arrives so she decides to go around the corner to the auxiliary lot. Khara spots a space in the rear of the yard she pulls in and realizes the blue sedan is right next to her.

After parking the Corvette she stands and looks around. There is no one walking by, and the city never installed any security cameras at the back lot due to budget cuts. With the knowledge evidence cars are always locked if they are not in a secured area, and there is no way to lock the car as she took the keys after the shootout, she opens the rear door. With her right hand reaching in she flips the back seat up, unzips her backpack, and takes out the disassembled sniper rifle placing the weapon on the floor where the back seat would be. With a quick flick, the seat is placed back in place and is now sitting over the assassination weapon she used.

Not seeing an N.Y.P.D. evidence sticker on the vehicle Khara is aware the car hasn't been gone over by the crime scene department yet. In a slick move, she takes the key out of her pocket, locks the car, and strolls back to the red Corvette.

The door to the Corvette is open, the empty backpack is flung into the trunk area of the car, and the black screen is pulled over the rear compartment blocking anyone from peeking inside the car. She hops in and starts the vehicle to move away from the blue sedan parking at the other end of the lot. Satisfied, Khara walks around the corner, and enters the precinct.

With a swagger to her step, and the taps of her boots announcing her presence she waves hi to the desk sergeant while entering the building.

"I am overjoyed to see you again Detective Bennet, did you come back today to say hello or shoot some more people?"

"Always great to see you too Sarge, did the crime lab come here to go over the blue sedan in the lot?"

"Not yet. They called, and said they will be here in a little while."

"Did anybody in the precinct bother to go through the shooters car before they arrive?"

"No, we had to call a flatbed truck to tow the vehicle to our back lot. The central Staten Island yard is full. The captain said to lock the car up, and wait for the lab guys to come here."

Khara knew they couldn't secure the car as she is in possession of the key. No one obviously bothered to inform the captain either. The officers who received the blue car in the parking lot did not enter anything into evidence because they saw nothing out in the open, and they left the shooters sedan as is. Khara thought they must have figured the car is parked in the back of the facility, and no one would bother with any bullet-ridden car in a police storage yard.

A little while later the crime scene officers walk in the front doors and ask to be taken to the blue sedan. The desk sergeant turns his head and stares at Khara.

"Detective Bennet would you be so kind as to escort them to the vehicle please?"

Khara, realizing the sarcasm in his voice ignores it.

"Sure Sarge, you guys come with me. It's around the corner in our back lot."

The van parks in front of the blue sedan, and they try to open the doors but they are locked. The lead officer of the unit asks if anyone brought the key to the car from the precinct.

"I took the key. Let me open the doors for you."

Technically she is not lying about taking the key. She never said they came from the precinct. The lab unit is not going to question her as the car is locked as protocol requires in an unsecured location, and she was identified in the precinct as a detective.

They start to go over the car with a fine tooth comb when one of them flips the rear seat over and finds a sniper rifle disassembled with a sight sitting on the floor. Khara makes a suggestion to the lab officer in charge.

"The guys who drove this car were trying to kill me. They were Mexicans, and they could have been here at the same time to shoot Ted Ferry. I am heading the investigation into his killing. Please check this rifle out to make sure if this is the one used in his assassination."

The unit grabs and bags the gun's parts while continuing to dust for fingerprints. After they are finished they pack up and head back to their lab. Once they drive out of the lot Khara heads over to Corvette and slips in the driver's seat intent on driving to the city to meet with Johanna.

On her way back to Manhattan a call is placed to Junior.

"Hey Junior it's Khara, I need something from you quickly."

"Sure whatever, keep me informed."

"The special sniper rifle your dad gave to me, I want another duplicate one like it. Also, I want the gun delivered tomorrow morning to my apartment in Brooklyn."

"Consider it done."

* * *

The underground parking garage at police headquarters stops her at the entrance. The office in charge meanders over to the red Corvette, and remembers her from the Mercedes AMG she took out and destroyed.

"Hello, again detective. Is this a trade you are bringing in here today? I saw what you did to the other car you took out last week."

"Kind of a trade I imagine. Do you want to park this or should I?"

"Depends if the Corvette is evidence or your personal vehicle?"

"Sort of both in a way I guess. I'll probably be taking it out again unless you can give me another hot car?"

"Funny, really funny, I'll park this for you. How long will you be?

"Not long, an hour or so. Be careful with it, please. It's not mine."

"I never would have guessed."

The driver's door opens and she hops out heading for the secured elevator area to go upstairs to Johanna's office.

With confidence, she opens the door to the deputy commissioner's office and marches in to be greeted by the receptionist.

"Please tell the commissioner Detective Bennet is here to meet with her."

"No need I am aware she is waiting for you Detective. Please knock and go in."

Khara finds her sitting behind her desk. Johanna is talking on the telephone and waves for her to sit on a small sofa in the office. Finally finished speaking she hangs up her phone and sits next to her on the sofa shoulder to shoulder.

"So tell me what your Russian landlords found out?"

"The FSB informed them the passports came out of Chechnya, and a rebel group is behind this whole thing. They sent the two Pupovich women here, and Olga and I are going to go to Grozny to find her. I need your backup with the CIA and Homeland Security."

"Consider the request taken care of. The passports were ordered right after I spoke to you on the phone, and I also called my Federal contacts. You are good to go, and I want you to be aware the CIA will be tracking you as best they can once you are on Russian territory."

"I will be leaving in a day or two for Moscow with Olga. I'll use my personal credit card and the department can reimburse me."

"No problem with getting paid back. Be careful."

Johanna leans in, hugs her goodbye, gives Khara a long lingering kiss, and she asks if there is time to join her for lunch.

"Why not, I'm starting to become hungry myself. Where do you want to go?"

"A few times I ate at a great steakhouse across from the New York Stock Exchange near Exchange Place. I'll ask my driver to take us to the restaurant now. Come on let's go."

The receptionist calls for a reservation notifies the downstairs lobby to release her official vehicle, and two detectives are again waiting for them in an unmarked police car.

The traffic going to the Wall Street area is heavy but flowing. The detectives drop them off a block away, and the two of them blend in with the crowds moving on the sidewalks and streets.

The entry to the restaurant opens by the bar with its warm wood tones and the back bar liquor bottles are glistening in subdued spotlighting. The hostess confirms their reservation and escorts them to a table by a side window. Menus are brought over, and they decide on what to eat as the waiter approaches them. Khara goes first.

"I'll order the sliced filet mignon sandwich topped with a mushroom sauce and fried onions."

The server asks if she would like fries on the side as they come with the sandwich.

"No, but I would like some onion rings please."

Johanna orders the twelve-ounce cheeseburger with toppings on it. Finished taking their order the waiter walks away, and Johanna tells Khara she will miss her and wishes she can go to Europe with her someday.

"Tell you what Johanna. How about when I come back we go on a vacation to Mexico. I can mix pleasure with business. I want to straighten out some things with the Mexican Secret Police."

"I'm sorry but I didn't hear anything you said. Remember if we go to Mexico together you can't tell me anything you do on your own. Do you understand what I am saying? I will cover for you as much as I can but there are some things I do not want to have any knowledge of."

"Johanna I might need a few days to myself if we go... nothing major. I am aware of the situation you are in."

"Understood, our food is coming let's enjoy it."

A few probing questions are asked of her during the course of the meal, and Khara answers guardedly.

"Do you want me to obtain the plane tickets for you and Olga?"

"No Olga is handling the arrangements, and she is making all the reservations through her Russian contacts."

"Oh, do you know who they are?"

"I have no idea. She will be paying for the airfare as far as I am aware. We can always reimburse her if you like."

"The CIA will handle all money issues. Let me know who they are seeing when they fly to Moscow. I want to make sure you are safe. I will ensure one of our embassy aids meet with the two of you when you arrive."

Khara isn't sure if she means what she is saying or is trying to finagle more information out of her. Either way, there is nothing she would say which might put her life in jeopardy. The old maxim loose lips sink ships applies to assassins too.

Coffee is ordered after the meal, and Johanna picks up the tab.

"I heard you are now driving a red Corvette. What happened to your BMW, and when did you purchase such a hot car?"

"Oh, I didn't buy it. The car belongs to the moron I shot on Plum Island. The second Popovich shot up the Mercedes AMG from the confiscated vehicles pound I borrowed so I loaned his Corvette to drive back to the city. I am waiting for my car to be finished being repaired, and after I can drive it again I'll turn this one into the department, and the Corvette can be considered confiscated property according to protocol."

"Please try not to hurt anyone with it if you can. The vehicle is still not entered into the department's computer system as confiscated."

They finish and walk outside looking for the detectives to pick them up. The unmarked car arrives to bring everyone back to headquarters. Johanna goes upstairs, and Khara walks into the garage to reclaim the red Corvette.

Khara asks for the car to be brought back and is told they are gassing it up for her and will be back in a minute or two. As soon as the officer said this to her she immediately knew he is lying. They can't fill the gas tank of an unauthorized vehicle. In her mind, she is thinking someone is either putting a listening device in the car or a tracker somewhere inconspicuous. From her days as an undercover drug officer, she is aware of what they can do, and what they can't. Now she will need to be careful about what she says in the car if she gets a phone call while in the Corvette.

Finally, her car is brought to the exit, and Khara is on her way back to Brooklyn via the Brooklyn Bridge.

The Corvette is stopped at the valet line by her building, and she tells the young boy not to move the car but to watch it for a few minutes. The doorman opens the massive glass etched entry door for her, and she asks the concierge to call Olga down to the lobby for a moment.

The wait feels like seconds to Khara.

Olga strolls out of the elevator, and asks Khara what she needs to speak to her about?

"I think the police or CIA planted a bug in the Corvette while I ate lunch today. I need your team to go through it, and make sure the car is clean."

In Russian, she speaks to the concierge and he calls over the two armed men in suits sitting in the lobby. One of them walks out and drives the Corvette away. Olga turns to Khara to inform her of the security measures the vehicle will go through.

"By dinner time the car will be cleaned of any listening or tracking devices. Relax we will take care of everything, nothing to worry about. Also, your M3 is repaired. The windows are replaced, and the broken glass removed from the interior of the car. Whenever you want your car the valet will bring it around for you."

"Thank you, I appreciate you and Viktor making the repairs for me."

"We are better than insurance. It costs you nothing. How about eating dinner with us tonight?"

"Not sure if I can. My fiancé might want to come over because I'll be going to Europe in a day or two with you, and not see him."

"I understand. Tomorrow the plane tickets will be sent to me by hand. We are scheduled to fly directly to Riga Latvia. There is some business I need to attend to before our contact will meet us, and we will take a train from the Baltic country to Moscow."

"Good and I am thinking maybe you should not clean the Corvette. We can use the bug in the car as a decoy in the future if we want to throw someone off our trail."

Olga smiles at the thought of misleading the authorities.

In Russian, she calls out to the concierge, and he uses his personal mobile phone to call the men who drove the Corvette away a few minutes before and relays her message. They smile and each goes in a different direction.

Khara walks back outside and takes her phone out of her rear pocket and calls Don.

"Hey Don interested in stopping by tonight to eat dinner with me?"

'Can't I am being sent out of town on an assignment."

"Too bad I was hoping to see you before I also went away. Where are they sending you?"

"Unfortunately Khara you know I can't say where this is a highly classified mission."

"I understand I'll miss seeing you."

"Me too, sorry, but I will make it up to you when I come back."

"I look forward to it Don, bye."

Not seeing him is not a real concern of hers. She only needs to touch base so as not to arouse suspicion. Not knowing where he is going is a concern and is starting to bug her, and why he never asked her where she is being sent also bothered her. Later in the evening, she begins to reflect on the conversation, and the thought crosses her mind he must be aware of where she is headed already so he did not need to ask.

Her thoughts are interrupted when her phone starts to vibrate in her palm. The screen lights up and looking down the caller ID pops Johanna's number up on the screen. It is a text message telling her tomorrow the passports will be hand delivered to Brooklyn early in the morning. She text her back with a quick thank you

Now realizing she still needs to pack Khara walks inside and goes to her apartment to put together what she will need. With a United States diplomatic passport she can pack her bags with the MP7 machine gun, ammunition and her grenades secure in the knowledge the suitcase cannot be searched, as well as her personal self.

With clothes in hand, she starts to fold her blouses when the concierge rings her on the intercom. Her partner Matt is downstairs and would like to come up to talk to her.

"Yes let him up, thank you."

In a few minutes, her doorbell rings, and she invites Matt inside.

"This is a good looking place Khara. I've never been here before, and the security in the building is overwhelmingly frightening."

"Yes, I am well aware of it. For the first time in a long time, I feel secure at home. What brings you around at this time of night? You are either working or with your family in Queens."

"I wanted to speak to you about the security guard you shot when we went to Plum Island. He was interviewed after he came out of surgery and I was present to hear his answers. The guard said he was paid a lot of money to recommend hiring Popovich, and try to steal the Persian Goat virus. The virus was stolen before he took what he thought is the toxin. What he held in his hand when he stood in the surf is colored water. The real virus is unaccounted for and missing, and he didn't know it."

"Did he say who hired him?"

"Yes, the biochemist Gretchen Popovich paid him in cash as a down payment. The guard told our interrogators if he could manage to travel off the island, and bring the vial home where she would be waiting for him he would never need to work again for the rest of his life. Now we recognize the reason he desperately wanted to leave the island."

"It is a false promise of money. Gretchen Popovich is a Chechen rebel leader, not a biochemist. The woman who we encountered at his home in Riverhead could not be the biochemist or the rebel leader. She wouldn't chance coming here and leave Russia, and not slip back in easily. The real biochemist, whoever in reality she is, is able to weaponize the virus, and more than likely is out of the country with the toxin by now. I'll bet the woman they left in the house in

Riverhead is a rebel soldier and is supposed to kill the laboratory guard to clean up any loose threads when he arrives home. With luck, we reached the house first."

"Makes sense to me. How do you know the real Popovich is a Chechen rebel leader?"

"Olga told me. Johanna spoke to Homeland Security and they confirmed the fact to her. I will be leaving as soon as my passport arrives. I'm flying to Moscow with Olga to find her."

"You be careful in Russia. They don't speak Spanish so watch your back."

"Don't worry Olga will be traveling with me. She told me we will be on Air Baltic to Riga International, and when we land we will meet an FSB agent, and take the train to Moscow."

"We'll be careful when you are there because I am used to you as a partner."

They hug and she escorts him to the door. As Khara opens the locks for him to leave the elevator opens, and an armed Russian guard approaches her apartment.

"Miss Bennet tomorrow you will be flying out to Riga. The tickets are here, and Olga is waiting for the passports to arrive tomorrow."

"Thank you, I appreciate the information. Tell her I am packing my bags."

***

Early the next morning Big Boy enters the lobby of Khara's apartment house and tells the concierge he is bringing a package for Detective Bennet. The protocol is to pick up the phone and calls upstairs. He informs her a large man is here with an unknown package. Immediately Khara understands who is in the lobby waiting for her, and what he is bringing. When she leaves the elevator and is greeted by him standing next to the concierge a broad smile crosses her face.

"Glad to see you, Biggie. I guess Junior was able to obtain what I asked him for yesterday."

"Junior had to pull a few strings but he was able to find one for you in Sterling Virginia. I drove down south last night to buy the rifle. I'm sure you'll use it well."

"Appreciate the effort, Biggie. Thank you."

With her package in tow, she goes backupstairs to eat breakfast.

About midmorning, the passports are hand-delivered to the building, and Khara is called down to the lobby to sign for them. After she is in possession of the books Olga is notified, and she also comes down to the main entrance to be handed her diplomatic passport.

"Khara tonight we fly to Riga. I booked a direct flight. Baltic Air will take a little over eight hours until we arrive. Bring some food with you as theirs may not be to your taste."

"Good to know. I think I'll visit the kosher delicatessen down the avenue and pick up two sandwiches for us. I bought some small insulated bags which will keep them fresh until we eat them."

Finished talking Khara turns to the front door and goes outside. The smell of salt water is refreshing in the morning. No car fumes or trucks idling. Not waiting for the crosswalk light to turn green she crosses the street to stroll on the boardwalk which runs parallel to Brighton Beach Avenue.

The sun is shining as she strolls on the wooden boards which appear to stretch out one after the other forever. The businesses on the esplanade are open, and people are stopping in to shop. Khara continues on until she reaches her side street and begins to ramble off the promenade to the avenue a few steps ahead. But as she approaches the down ramp there are a few young boys sitting on the boardwalk railings, and they call out to her.

"Hey, chica you want to party with us today?"

Not one to back down Khara stops and walks back toward them. In an instant, she grabs the chain around her neck and flips her gold shield out to lie across her chest so they will see it. They appear to her to be about fourteen years old, and some of them still have peach fuzz on their faces with only a wisp of dark hair on their upper lip. A flashback to years ago when she did undercover narcotics work in Brooklyn came to mind.

The commissioner asked her to speak to a junior high school in Spanish Harlem which, at the time, is out of her district about drugs, and instructed to wear her blues. The police department wanted young impressionable children to see a minority female in uniform to try to inspire them to go into law enforcement.

It was about June and the eighth graders were graduating, and going on to high school. This was to be an inspirational speech she gave, and when finished she goes to her car when one of the young boys from the audience stands in front of her asking for a dollar.

Khara remembers staring at him, but he stood his ground and did not move aside.

"Move or I'll move you. I don't have time for this nonsense."

The young boy held his ground and did not budge.

"C'mon officer, give me a dollar. You can afford it."

"If you are smart you'll listen to me. Go to high school and get an education so you won't need to beg people for money."

Khara felt she must have struck a nerve with him as she thought he didn't think of this as begging.

The young boy stood still, allowed her to walk around him, and enter her squad car to drive away. The time must be two years later or so when she saw his junior high school picture in the newspaper. He was shot dead in a bad drug deal outside his high school in the Bronx.

She hears the boy's accent and starts to speak Spanish to the group.

"You don't realize how lucky you are, but I am not going to kill any you today."

With a slow movement she slides her leather jacket open exposing her gold detective's shield and her holstered weapon.

"How old are you young wanna-bees?"

"Two of us are fourteen, he is fifteen."

"I want you to walk off the boardwalk and go home. If I see you out of school again I am going to arrest you, and your mothers will need to go to court to explain to a judge and social services why you should be allowed to live back home and not in the youth jail."

The boys give a disgruntled expression on their face; they slide off the railing and walk off the boardwalk. Khara follows them to the Avenue and when they continue on the side street she turns left and goes a few doors down to the delicatessen to buy her food.

Upon opening the door to the store she enters, and the counterman recognizes her, and in his best Brooklyn accent with a smile on his face asks her a question she has heard before.

"Hey, detective are you here today to eat or kill someone?"

"Sorry, it is not noon yet. Guess I'll have to wait till after lunch before I start shooting."

"I'm glad to hear it. What'll you have?"

"Two corn beef on rye with mustard, sour pickles, and some potato salad to go, and four cans of Doctor Browns Black Cherry soda."

"You got it. Give me a minute, and I'll pack everything up for you."

The petite elderly white-haired waitress who is always working in the delicatessen wants to say hello to her, and makes her way up to the front of the store by the counter, taking small slow steps.

"You're not eating in today sweetie?"

"No, I have to pack for a short trip with a friend. But I'll be back soon."

With a twinkle in her eye, she looks up at Khara.

"I hope the friend is good looking. To be honest I only travel with a handsome one, or two, also."

Chapter Six

A dark burgundy sedan with federal license plates stops at the yellow valet line in front of the apartment house. The driver stays inside while two men exit, and start to walk to the entrance of the building. Dressed in dark blue suits they look like cookie cutter federal law enforcement agents of some kind. Clean cut with a short haircut wearing dark aviator style sunglasses. The doorman, in a thick Russian accent, asks what their business is before he will let them in.

One of the men flips his wallet open, and a CIA badge and photo identification are shown. "We are here to speak to Detective Bennet."

The deep etched front glass door opens, and they walk into the lobby as the doorman continues to watch them pass him, and enter where the concierge again asks for their identification. Satisfied he rings upstairs to Khara and announces the visitors to her.

"Tell them I will be down in a minute, and to wait for me by the curb."

Khara throws on her leather jacket, takes the elevator down to the lobby, and walks outside to where the men are waiting on the sidewalk. Again they flip open their identification, and before they are given a chance to say anything she speaks first.

"Follow me across the street to the boardwalk, and don't say a word."

Nobody is speaking as the three walk onto the wooden planks, and they only go about twenty feet or so when Khara stops by the iron railing. She leant against the cool metal with her back to the water. This will make her talking almost impossible for anyone except her to listen to what they are saying as they are speaking into the wind, and the sound of the crashing ocean waves muffles their speech.

The two men inch closer to her, and the taller one begins to speak.

"The CIA is aware you are going to Russia on a diplomatic passport, and why. Our embassy in Moscow assigned someone to stay far behind, and trail you at a distance for your safety. In case you should want some assistance he will be close by to help."

"Tell me how will I recognize who he is if I should need him?"

"Our agent will approach you, and he will tell you 'dead girls don't die,' remember the code."

"This must be one of the stupidest coded words I ever heard, and you want me to keep these words in mind?"

"Our intelligence department suggested using this phrase because Popovich died twice yet is still not dead. In Russia, the FSB plants internal domestic spies everywhere. Our advice to you is trust nobody. Your life will depend on being vigilant, and they don't care if you live or die."

The two CIA agents turn away leaving her standing alone on the boardwalk watching them as they cross the street, and drive off in their vehicle.

The alarm on her phone begins to vibrate, and she knows she needs to hustle back upstairs to retrieve her bags. It is almost time to leave.

Once in her apartment she makes sure she places on her person the two guns, the throwing knife is in her boot, and the hand grenade she always now carries is in her small sling pocketbook. The stuff laying on the bed she grabs, and places the sandwiches and soda into a freezer bag, and inside the outside pocket of the brown backpack which is carrying clothes, and her MP7 machine gun.

A limousine with Viktor sitting in the back is waiting downstairs for the two women, and in short order, they are ensconced in the back seat being driven to Kennedy International Airport. After walking into the central terminal they are directed to the airline office to check in with their diplomatic identification thus allowing them to board without being searched for weapons.

Both women are cleared to enter the gate area when Olga's phone rings. Viktor is calling. After a short conversation with him, she turns to Khara.

"Turn around we are not going to Riga or Russia. Walk with me outside, and I will tell you why."

With their bags in tow, they go back out to the arrivals sidewalk, and she calls for her limo to return and pick them up. They are standing at the end of the terminal where no one else is when Olga starts to explain what Viktor told her.

"My old contact at the FSB reached out to us only a few minutes ago. We are on a wild goose chase. Popovich is in America, not Chechnya."

"Do you trust him, and his information?"

"Honestly I can tell you I know him for many years, intimately. My special friend and I grew up in the same orphanage in Russia. Back when I was in high school I dated a boy whose father at the time is a Jewish commissar which is highly unusual. After classes, we would go into the woods to engage in quiet time together with no one bothering us. One day this older policeman followed us, and he shot my boyfriend. The commissar previously demoted him from the rank of captain back to a private, and he killed my teenage lover for revenge. The officer killed him in cold blood."

"What did you do when he murdered him?"

"In a hurry, I gathered up my clothes from the grass because the shot attracted people, and they are running to where my friend and I were in the woods. The officer looked at my naked body, and he told me to be at the corner of the orphanage at night because he will be waiting for me. The officer said if I do not come when he parks the police car he will kill me tomorrow like he killed my boyfriend. I ran out of the woods as fast as I could and didn't look back. At the time there is no choice for me but to go with him, I am going to meet the officer after dark."

"So you snuck out when he arrived?"

"Yes everyone is sleeping. I am sitting by my bedroom window at night, and I am looking for him to arrive. The car parked down the road and blinked its headlights so I knew this must be him. In a hurry, I went down the back stairway through the kitchen. On my way out I grabbed a steak knife and slid the blade in my sock with the point facing down. The rear door opened without squeaking, and I ran down the block as quickly as I could, and jumped in the back of the police car. The fat pig drove me through an original growth wooded forest for a while until he came to an old abandoned woodcutter's shack. The car is parked, and he turned off the engine. The area is pitch black out except for the illumination from a full moon. The driver's door opened, and he slid out of the car, followed by his opening the rear door where I am sitting. The only light shining in the windows is from the sky above. The one thing I remember is how dark out the woods are, totally, and nobody is around who would be able to help me. The policeman is now standing by the door undressing on the side of the dirt road when he told me to undress also. The officer is armed so I did as I am ordered for fear of my life. His gun is still outside with his uniform, but now on the ground."

"Anxious to screw me in haste he climbed in the back of the police car with his unwashed body smelling like a stable, and his repulsive cigar breadth only inches from my face. The piece of shit began to kiss my body when I reached down below the seat, grabbed the steak knife in my left hand, and started to stab him in the neck twisting the shaft as best I could. Bracing my legs against the rear door pillars I grabbed his thick hair with my right hand as I continued to thrust my blade into his throat. Each time I stabbed him he screamed out, but yelling didn't help him. In the middle of a forest, nobody is out at night who can hear him yell except for the animals. Soon he will be a dead policeman too. My first kill is for revenge."

"The blood from his neck gushed all over the rear seat and my body. With blood streaming all over the place he is straining to back out of the police car. Since I am a long-distance runner, and athletic my legs had the strength to keep him in the car for a little while longer as I tried to kill him. The back seat became too slippery from the assholes blood, and I started to slide out of the car holding his hair with a death grip in my hand. Soon he stopped moving, and I turned over to dump his body off me, and onto the floor of the car. At last, I let go of the knife and the blade remained in his neck. His bloody body landed on my clothes so I tugged as hard as I could, and grabbed them all. Naked I ran all the way back to the orphanage as fast as I could. The cool night air invigorated me, and the distance didn't bother me."

"The FSB agent I grew up with in the orphanage knew who I am going to see because I confided in him, and I told him my plan before I left at night. He met me at the rear kitchen door when I returned, and let me back in the building. He helped wash my body down with warm wet rags, and remove the blood from me. The time is now early in the morning so I couldn't take a chance of a shower so late at night. About an hour later we are done cleaning me up and he took my clothes to place them in a dumpster with the garbage. After the night is over he became my second lover until both of us together joined the Russian Army when we finished school. So yes I trusted him with my life in the past, and I still do now."

"So where the hell is Popovich, did he obtain new information?"

"Viktor said he will tell me more when we go back to the penthouse."

The limo stops by them, and both hop in the back seat to be returned to Brooklyn.

***

The two women leave the elevator and enter Olga's apartment. Viktor is talking on the telephone sitting in his lounge chair writing something on a pad in Russian.

"Welcome back ladies. Glad I saved you a long trip for nothing. Your old orphanage buddy contacted me, and he said Popovich is somewhere in the western part of the United States. The FSB is following her as best they can because she is the leader of a Chechen rebel group. He asked for you to contact him on a secure line."

"What kind of hack-proof phone do you use Olga?"

"The KGB gave us a coded phone line years ago which scrambles the sounds. Unless you enter the exact code on the other side you will never be able to listen into the conversation. My friend and I use the street address of the orphanage plus both of our room numbers as our secret passwords. The two of us are the only people alive who remember our room numbers. Not Viktor or anyone else can pry the secret code out of me, and he on many occasions tried. Give me a minute I will call him now."

She walks into a side room where she maintains a private office. The door closes behind her, and Khara listens as a deadbolt turns to lock her inside the room. In a few minutes, Olga comes out and tells them what she was told.

"Popovich is tied in with a band of Alt-right militias in Colorado. The women used her identification to sneak a few of her rebels into the country to steal a certain virus which originates in the hills of Iran. The American militias financed her revolutionary group, and the Times Square terrorism is how they tested and tried the toxins out. If the assault worked the plan is the Chechnya rebels would use the airborne poison in Moscow and other cities in the knowledge the Russian FSB laboratories would blame Iran's crazy Revolutionary Guard for the killings. The Kremlin would, in turn, retaliate against Iran and take over their oil fields. Popovich knew the Ayatollahs would counter-attack, and this would leave Russia in a weakened state so Chechnya could revolt, and rise again as an independent country after the dust settled."

Khara is standing in the middle of the room digesting all this information. Now she realizes why the Times Square terror attack took place. The FSB contact told her not to go to Russia after Popovich because she is here in the states.

"I'm going downstairs to my place to call Johanna. She is the deputy commissioner of terrorism, and might possess more knowledge on the militias than your source does."

The ride down takes only a few minutes before she is in her apartment, and on the phone.

"Johanna I am not going to Russia. Long story short Popovich is in Colorado with a militia group. The right-wing crazies are the ones who financed the terror attack in the city. What militias are you aware of in the Rockies, and where are they based? I need to fly out as soon as possible."

"A few militias are in the west and I am certain where they are located. The most vociferous and dangerous of them is the POC militia in Colorado."

"Never heard of them, Johanna. What does POC stand for?"

"Protect Our Constitution. The group is recruiting in all the right-wing and militia magazines. They are involved in the takeover of the Federal building in Montana this past summer. The FBI and federal marshals stormed the place because they took hostages, and when they fired an RPG at a perimeter barricade outside the building they decided negotiations are futile. The standoff became a real bloodbath."

"Does the department possess any idea where in Colorado they might be located? My foreign source told me Popovich is tied in with them. I'll fill you in later."

"Okay I'll book a flight to Denver for you, and I'll try to make arrangements for today. I'll email you the ticket confirmation. The latest info we obtained on the POC is they set up a major cell in Central Oak Creek Colorado. I'll text you the address when I hang up the phone."

"Also I need one for Olga. She speaks a few languages plus Russian in case I want her to translate for me if I meet with Popovich, so she should come with me. Do you know where Don is? He told me he will be away on an assignment, but he couldn't tell me, are your contacts cognizant of his whereabouts?"

"Sorry Khara, you are aware Homeland Security keeps information on FBI agent assignments confidential, and on a need to know basis."

"Yes I figured as much, but no harm in asking. Also, did you find out anything about the two Mexicans who tried to kill me by the toll plaza?"

"Yes, they are in the country illegally. The impostors are not carrying any legal visas or papers on them, nor can I find any in the computer system. The CIA thinks they are related to Ted Ferry's assassination because our lab crew found the sniper rifle they used to kill him in their car. The caliber of the gun fits the bullet we dug out of the steps at city hall and a ballistics test confirmed it."

"Glad you found out who shot him. Guess I'm off the case since this mystery is settled. Also, you do remember I needed to go to Mexico after this is over to try and settle this Ecru Cartel crap once and for all. I'm tired of them always following me, and trying to kill me all the time."

"We can talk about a vacation south of the border when you get back to New York. Is there anything else you need before you leave?"

"No, I'm all packed and ready to go. I'm waiting for the airline tickets you are going to send to hit my email."

"Okay, I'll take care of this immediately. Have a good flight, and try not to kill too many people."

After she hung up Khara started to think about the Ecru Cartel and the Colonel from the secret police who is now running the drug operation. Her thinking is "if they followed me in the blue sedan once, I am sure they will attempt to kill me again. The Colonel will not give up until I am dead."

Dialing Olga, she tells her the plan is to go to Colorado and asks if she would like to take an all-expense paid adventure with her. Of course, the answer is positive.

***

With her arms slung through the time-worn backpack, and it sitting securely on her back she grabs her small suitcase taking the elevator down to the lobby. Olga again arranged for her limousine to drive them to Newark Liberty Airport in New Jersey. The ride across Staten Island is in heavy bumper to bumper traffic and continues over the Goethals Bridge to Elizabeth.

The limousine drives up the departure ramp and drops them off by Terminal C. Their luggage is minimal so they take it in themselves, and head for the airline office to check in with their diplomatic passports. Cleared to board they enter the passenger boarding area without being searched and head to their gate to wait for the flight to leave. Khara looks at her phone and realizes she needs to kill about forty minutes till the gateway door opens for boarding. Leaving her backpack and a small suitcase with Olga she heads for the restroom down the hallway.

Located in the New York area there are a lot of Spanish speaking people in the terminal either working or flying as passengers. Fluent in the language Khara listens to what they are saying and ignores their conversations as she turns to go in the women's restroom, and enters a stall. Before she does she stops to check her makeup and looks in the mirrors on the wall facing the line of bathroom stalls. A woman is standing off to the side right behind her and in front of an empty stall. Khara takes notice of the middle-aged Mexican girl slide her coat open, and her hand goes back and grasps the handle of a pistol sitting holstered on her hip.

In a lightning quick move Khara turns, and with a high kick strikes the woman in the chest repelling her backward onto the toilet in the stall. Rushing in between the blue-gray steel walls she pins the woman's neck with her right hand against the yellow rear tiled wall making her eyes to start to bulge out. A look of sheer panic crosses the woman's face as the thin metal door slams shut behind them with Khara looming over her.

The blunt force of the kick knocked the wind out of the woman causing her to not have enough strength to tear away Khara's death grip on her neck. The woman's lips start to turn blue from lack of air so she loosens the tight grasp on her airway, and the woman sits back gasping for breath.

Knowing the answer before she asks, the question is given to her in Spanish.

"Who sent you here to kill me? Tell me now or you will die a painful death."

"The Colonel ordered us to New York to finish you off. He is afraid of you. Your reputation in the Ecru

Cartel is legendary because you killed so many of his men."

"How many are of you are following me today?"

"Three of us are here. The Colonel wanted us to kill you, and we are tracking after you for a few weeks. No, I am not aware of the identities of the others. But the two men look like gringos, and not Mexican like me."

Khara reaching down inside the woman's cardigan sweater she lifts the woman's pistol up and slides the magazine clip out from the gun placing it in her own jacket. To do this she needs to release her grip on the woman's neck giving the assassin a chance to recover her strength. With no warning the woman head butts Khara in the groin area forcing her body to slam backward against stall door slamming it shut.

With a loud bang, the thin metal door reverberates as Khara hits her head against the steel missing the chrome clothes hook protruding out a few inches. Rebounding into the stall Khara punches the sitting woman several times hitting her in the face using all her body weight behind her fist smashing her nose flat like a pancake. Blood is pouring out of the stunned woman's face as Khara reaches down to her boot, and withdraws her throwing knife.

Striking her with a few quick slashes to the throat the woman starts to gurgle and drown in her own blood as her body goes limp. After wiping the blade clean on the dying woman's clothes she forces the assassin's pistol down between her legs into the toilet, turns to open the stall door, and exits closing it behind her.

Still, in need of a restroom, she travels further into the terminal to use the next one. This time the area is empty, and no incident occurs. Finished she walks back to Olga and sits next to her on the curved dark blue vinyl seat.

"Did you see anything interesting on your way to the restroom Khara?"

"Yes, I only needed to kill one lady who the Colonel sent after me. The dead assassin told me two more are here, and she said they don't look like Mexicans."

"Not a problem. When we find out who they are we will deal with them."

An announcement is made by the airline ticket agent at the door boarding will begin in a minute or two. After they walk down the airport corridor together to board the airplane Olga takes her seat in the row right behind where Khara is sitting. This enables her to protect her from any rear attack.

The heavy door to the plane closes, the lever is pulled down to lock it shut, and the passengers are all seated and buckled in for takeoff. With everyone ready, the stewardess explains the emergency procedures while the man who is next to Khara looks out the window past the person sitting next to it. Seeming nervous he turns to Khara while white-knuckling the armrest.

"Excuse me do you fly often? You appear so relaxed."

Most of the time Khara does not control her patience well so she answers him as expected.

"No, I don't."

"Are you going to Denver to ski or on business?"

"Business."

"What kind of business are you in?"

Inpatient and wanting to sit back and close her eyes she decides to end the conversation in a hurry.

With her left hand, she pulls her leather jacket back in a casual way exposing a little of her Sig Sauer to him.

"My business is killing terrorists, and people who annoy me too much."

"Oh, I'm sorry to bother you."

The rest of the flight he either reads or naps, and does not speak to her at all. The flight arrives on time and the landing is uneventful. Olga and Khara managed to take their bags on the plane with them so they do not need to go to baggage claim.

Central Oak Creek is about three hour's west on I-70 and north on State Route 9. Khara leases a four-wheel drive SUV which is high enough to go off road if needed. Both of them throw their luggage in the back, she jumps up into the driver's seat and heads out of the airport.

The route is picturesque with the mountains jutting into the sky with nothing but fields of green trees on both sides of the highway. The SUV turns off the interstate to route 9, and the scenery starts to become more rustic.

Going over the mountains the road levels out as they arrive in Central Oak Creek. A quaint old western burgh nestled in a valley with a small population of a few hundred people, and as many horses and four-wheel drive vehicles. The street is devoid of pedestrians with almost no traffic on the broad roads as they head to the only hotel in town, which is named The Hotel. It is located off Main Street as you enter going north. Khara pulls her vehicle into the rear parking lot, and they empty the back seat heading into the hotel lobby with their gear to check in.

Reminding her of old western pictures is the required overhanging balcony out front with thin oak posts holding it up. The sidewalk is also wood, and creeks when they walk on it stepping up from the asphalt street.

Olga enters first followed by Khara as they go in and head straight to the retro 1950's check-in desk. It is a wooden counter with a worn looking thick oak board on top. The desk clerk is behind it facing the old fashion mail box slots.

They approach closer to register and the clerk does not turn around until Khara says hello. The front desk clerk turns to greet them, and it is Don Weber.

The lobby is empty at the moment with only a few people in the attached restaurant off to the side.

"What are you two doing here?"

"Do you think maybe I could also ask you the same thing?" Khara said.

"This is a dangerous place to be. It is crawling with militia all over this town, they are armed, and waiting to use their weapons. The FBI placed me here, I am working undercover, and I don't need you two here interfering."

"Don't worry I promise you we won't be in your way."

"Don't make promises you can't keep Khara. I would like you two to go back home now."

"You do realize we can't leave here for the same reason you can't leave here."

"I am not happy about your staying so please be careful, and here are the keys to two rooms upstairs in the back. It is quieter at night in the rear of the hotel. Try to stay out of trouble, but knowing you I doubt you will be able to do it."

Khara ignores his plea and acts as if she does not hear him.

"Okay, thank you, sir. First, we are going to grab a bite to eat before going to our rooms. Is the food in your restaurant edible?"

"If you stick to burgers or eggs it is."

"Thanks for your suggestion."

The cafe is not too busy so they settle in at a round table in the rear by the back wall. The tables are covered with a red and white checkered plastic cloth, and the small wooden chairs with a slight curve in the back so they can enjoy some comfort for a short while.

Khara, as usual, sits with her back against the floral papered wall, and Olga is next to her also facing out to the entrance. A stocky fifty-something blond waitress wearing a pink uniform two sizes too small comes to the table and hands them a menu. Khara speaks up first.

"No thanks we don't need it; we'll each order a cheeseburger and fries well done. Do you serve any beer in this place?"

"In the mountains, we only serve American brewed Coors on tap, want one?"

"Sure why not."

"Twelve or twenty-ounce glass?"

"Make it twenty please for both of us"

The waitress leaves to go into the kitchen and returns in a minute with their beers. "The burgers will be out soon."

Olga sits back and starts to sip the ice cold beer served in a frozen mug. "I'm surprised the glass is frosted, I didn't expect anyone to do this in the middle of nowhere."

"Me too, I think it is a nice touch," Khara said.

A young man who appears to be in his mid-twenties with chiseled facial features, a short beard, wearing a camouflage baseball cap and a red plaid flannel shirt approaches their table.

"Mind if I join you?"

Olga does not respond. She doesn't want anyone to hear her Russian accent yet so Khara answers him.

"Not at all, pull up a chair."

"In this mountain area of Colorado, we don't get many visitors here much. To be honest with you two good looking women like you are rare in these parts."

"Thank you for the compliment."

This is not New York, and for a tall thin brunette white lady to be with an African American woman wearing a short afro haircut in the middle of the Rockies is most unusual, and the young man can't help but stare at them.

"What are you two doing here, are you big city lesbians slumming in the mountains?"

Not missing a beat Khara answers him.

"No, we are two bad ass women here to protect our constitution."

While she is saying these words Khara pulls her jacket back showing her Sig Sauer while Olga lifts her skirt up over her knee revealing the bottom of her holstered forty-five strapped to her muscular thigh.

"Oh, I see. How did you learn about this town in the middle of nowhere?"

"From a website the POC maintains. We decided we want to join, and stop those political traitors in Washington from giving our country to the liberal assholes on both coasts."

"Well let me make a phone call later tonight. If everything works out I'll meet you in the lobby tomorrow morning at ten. In case I'm not here to pick you up they don't want you."

"I want you to be aware both of us are excellent marksmen and experienced in hand to hand combat."

"I'll pass the information along. What room numbers are you two staying in?"

"Why are you interested in a visit tonight?"

"Could be."

"I'm in 205 in the rear and don't be too late. After flying into Denver today I need my beauty sleep, and I also must take a shower."

***

By the next morning, the young man is gone from Khara's room, and both women go downstairs to the restaurant for breakfast. Khara orders her usual coffee and buttered roll while Olga wants her eggs over easy, bacon well done with whole wheat buttered toast, and tea.

"So how did your late night visitor do Khara? The walls are paper thin and I heard everything."

Smiling at Olga she said "he's picking us up about ten thirty. We are going to meet with the militia somewhere in the mountains at a compound they built."

"First thing is we must find out where they keep their munitions. Afterwards, we will deal with Popovich."

"Not an issue, I told him we can obtain access to military grade weapons on the black market. Whatever they need we can acquire through our contacts."

"How did you convince him so fast?"

"Opened my backpack and I unpacked my new sniper rifle and scope. He never saw one like it before. When I took out my NATO MP7 he is now convinced we can obtain any munitions or arms they might want."

"Makes our task easier I guess. Here come my eggs, we'll talk later."

After breakfast, they walk out to the lobby, and Don calls them over to the registration desk to speak to them in private in a low whisper.

"So are you two leaving? The FBI is doing a major undercover operation going on here, and you are going to end up in the middle of it."

"Don, you are here for the POC militia aren't you?"

"Yes, after they took control of the federal building we are intent on disassembling them."

"Well, we are not after them as a first priority. Popovich is a rebel leader from Chechnya; she is with them, and being financed by the militia to develop a virus they both want to share for their own reasons. She is the one I am after. Homeland Security is backing me on this operation."

A black SUV pulls up to the curb and blows its horn three times. Olga turns to look outside and tells Khara their ride is here, and they must go now.

"I need to leave Don, I'll see you later."

"Be careful please, I don't want to be engaged to another woman if something happens to you. Once is enough for me."

The two walk out the front door and hop in the SUV with the young man from last evening.

"Good morning ladies, nice to see you two up, and ready to go. This morning we are headed into the mountains to our base camp. In a few minutes, we will arrive at our compound, you will be interviewed, and either accepted into the group or killed."

Khara is sitting next to him in the front seat, and she answers him in a blunt manner and tone of voice.

"I'm not easy to kill. In my past are plenty of dead men in Hell who can testify to what I said, believe me."

"After last night I don't doubt anything you tell me Khara. I'm only the messenger, and I do not make any major decisions."

"Who makes those decisions if you don't?"

"You will find out when we arrive. Now sit back and enjoy the scenery because we are going off road in a mile or so."

At the bottom of a hill, they make a left, and he turns off the highway onto an unpaved path which is only wide enough for one vehicle to travel on at a time as brush scrapes against the sides of the SUV. The ground underneath the SUV is rutted with puddles of rainwater splashing up onto the running boards and side windows. The dirt road twists and turns and comes to a divide when another left is made at another split but keeps going. The floor of the forest is dark due to the heavy tall tree growth. At one point the SUV flashes its headlights four times as a signal as camouflaged and armed men with automatic weapons appear out of the brush to wave them on.

At the top of the mountain, he makes a right turn into a small clearing. On the edges of the area, Khara recognizes camouflaged tents set back in the forest. From an airplane or helicopter flying overhead the base camp is almost invisible. Unless an infrared camera is used no one will ever realize a small army is based on the top of this hill.

The SUV stops under a large camouflage mesh net spread between many massive tall trees. Stepping out of the vehicle Khara and Olga stands and start to look around. A few feet away is a group of armed men, and a few women, sitting under another net listening to someone give a lecture on how to assault a building.

Khara can sense a battle brewing. Maybe not here, maybe not today, but the vibes in her body are tingling as her adrenaline is pumping, and she is certain it is coming.

Chapter Seven

Khara follows the young driver step by step into the woods, with Olga close behind. She can hear the distinctive crackling of gunshots in the distance followed by an explosion. Curious what weapons they are using she asks what they shooting with for practice.

"The POC militia uses an M16 carbine, mortars, and we use a rotation for incoming recruits on the firing range. For a firearms instructor, the unit hired a retired army sergeant and a patriot; Sarge is our trainer for the past three years. All newcomers need to go through our base camp program. In training, we believe no exclusions are valid because we want to be certain our militia know how to defend our constitution."

"The process makes sense to me. Guess we will also go through the basics."

"You will, only a handful of people were excused in the past due to their previous occupation."

Olga finally speaks and utters a quick comment to the young driver about the training making sense to her. Taken back upon hearing her accent he comments on it.

"Sorry I didn't know you were not an American. Where are you from?"

"Originally my birthplace is somewhere in Russia, and I have been in this country for many years, and am a proud American citizen now. Many years ago when I was a young girl I was in the Russian Army."

"Coincidentally we also have some Russians training here with us. Later when we are finished we can all meet for dinner and you can speak to them?"

"Yes, I would appreciate your introducing me to them. How many Russians are here?"

"There are a handful of men, including two women. Let us walk over behind the enormous tent and you can learn how we train our militia in hand to hand combat. The POC is lucky to employ a retired Marine Captain who has real fighting experience doing the training."

The three of them saunter over to the tent and follow him to a small clearing where four canvas mats are laid out on the ground. A group of eight white men is being instructed in hand to hand combat techniques by the trainer. Khara scrutinizes the Captain's size, estimates he is in his late forties, a bit over six foot with a flat top haircut, in shape and muscular. In her head, the words "typical Marine" comes to mind.

The escort calls out to the captain to come over when they approach the trainees, and he makes the introductions. With a scar running down the right side of his face he is an imposing figure. Khara perceives the officer is not thrilled to train females for warfare after hearing the tone of his voice as he gives a cursory hello. He visually inspects both of the women when he begins to question them.

"Did either of you ever engage in any hand to hand combat training?"

"In New York City I taught Krav Maga, and my friend learned hand to hand fighting in Russia when she was in their army," Khara said.

Now he is looking at her, and Khara thinks the captain is asking her a question with disdain in his voice. "Why don't you come onto the mat, and we can show the men a little demonstration. What do you say, sweetheart?"

In the past, she dealt with pig-headed assholes, and Khara cannot refuse the invitation. Her heart is starting to pump quicker; she is ready.

"Captain, can you give me a moment so I can put my weapons down and disarm?"

"Why should I? In the real world you would be fully armed if you were in combat, are you scared of getting your nails dirty?"

"Have it your way, let's go at it."

She is stepping on the mat as the instructor without warning pushes her as she places her right foot on the mat, and she lands on the dirt off the practice area. Khara is now pissed off at him.

"If you want to play this way Captain let's make it interesting."

"What do you have in mind girly?"

"Only one of us walks off alive."

The Captain is very tall, is looking down at her, and he is taken back by her brazen attitude. For a moment he is quiet. With a gruff voice, he answers her with a demand.

"In a life or death struggle, anything goes. Are you still game, or are you chickening out?"

"Anything goes is okay with me but I want you to remember you are the one who made the rules."

"Come on sweetie this is going to be a quick street fight."

The captain does not know she is a trained killer and a psychopath. The instructor backs up two feet and is standing in the middle of the mat waiting for her to come back on the padding.

Before stepping on the matt again she gives him a chance to back out.

"Hey, Captain I want to make sure you understand your rules. This is going to be a life or death struggle, and anything goes, correct?"

"Stop talking like a little girl already, and let's get at it. You're pissing me off now."

Khara turns to her escort before she does anything.

"Remember he said this is a street fight, and anything goes. I'm going to kill him."

With her eyes peeled on his, she steps back on the mat as he takes a step forward and throws a punch at her face. Khara slides to the side, with her left hand she pushes his arm downwards and proceeds to pound him in the middle of his face with her right hand following up with a lightening fist to his jaw with her left hand.

His nose broken and jaw is now dislocated to the side of his face. Blood is pouring down his chin as he staggers for a moment to clear the cobwebs and turns to face her again. The Captain raises his arms in a defensive stance, and this time he approaches with caution. He leads with a right foot kick. Khara again steps to the side, grabs his foot by the ankle with her left hand as his foot is raised, and swivels in toward him and quickly, with all her strength, throws two jabs to the front of his throat.

The Captain is gagging as he falls to the floor trying to catch his breath while his trachea collapses from the deadly hits to the middle of his throat. Khara turns to the group of men standing and watching.

"The lesson here is it doesn't matter what size asshole you encounter you can still kill him, remember this when you leave here."

The young escort runs over to the captain, peers down at him, and pivots to Khara.

"Will he be okay? The militia needs him for training our men."

Olga places her hand casually over her skirt and touches her gun which is strapped to her thigh underneath.

Khara is standing off the mats now and calmly answers the question.

"His surviving depends on if his trachea swells to heal itself from the hard impact of my punches. He will die if it contracts from suffocation by cutting off the airway. Or you can do an emergency field tracheotomy, and try to save his life. I can shoot him to finish him off if the tracheotomy cut in his throat doesn't work... your choice."

"Unfortunately we don't maintain any medical staff here, and the only hospital is about an hour or so away."

"Sucks to be him; the odds are he doesn't survive, and I personally don't think he will. Hire me, and I would be willing to train your men in hand to hand combat so they can win in a physical fighting situation."

Four young men rush onto the mat, lift the captain up, and carry him to his tent by his arms and legs.

"Well, I guess you are our new trainer Khara, welcome aboard. Both of you come with me and I'll show you where you two will be staying. To be honest with you I'm surprised you came out of the fight alive. I'm sure everyone thought you would be the one carried off."

"This jerk isn't the first person to underestimate me, and not live to tell about it."

"After watching you I believe everything you say. Over to the right, down this path, is the tent you two will be staying in while you are here."

"Listen I don't do tents well. I will stay at the hotel, and you can pick me up every morning. I like my luxuries, and have a hard time giving them up."

"We'll need to talk about this later. Tonight I can always bring both of you back for your things. Meanwhile, I think while you are here you will enjoy our meals. The food consists of farm fresh beef or lamb and cooked on an open grill. It's almost lunch so let's go over to the mess tent and grab a bite to eat. Also, I will introduce you to our Russian guests."

The dining area is an open-air clearing under the forest's high tree canopy. Another camouflage net is spread between the branches with picnic tables and benches scattered below for them to sit and eat. The meal today is organic chicken raised by a local farmer and barbecued on a stone-lined wood-fired grill.

"Grab a plate and we'll go by the larger red table on the edge of the clearing."

Everyone is picking up plates, and dinnerware as they stand in line to select their food and go to sit with their escort at a table on the far side of the area.

A full keg of Colorado-brewed Coors beer is tapped into, and a glass pitcher is brought over to their table for them.

While eating and engaging in small talk their escort is interrupted a few times and asked questions which he answers with authority. This leads Khara to believe he is not only a young stud who she slept with last night but someone higher up the food chain. Always curious she turns to him and asks an important question.

"So tell me who runs this outfit anyway?"

"The POC unit on this mountain I am in charge of until relieved. For security reasons, our commander speaks to his leaders by phone instead of in person when he needs to communicate with us. Nobody is sure of his identity due to the FBI and CIA trying to arrest him."

"Where do you store your weapons? We would like to inspect what else you are using, and if we need to supplement it."

"After lunch, I'll take to over to our weapon depot. The POC is developing a new bioweapon which we tested recently. If we can make enough supplies of it we will be a force to be reckoned with as we take back America from the left wing liberals in Washington. At the moment our new secret weapon is in limited quantities. The physical supply depot for this militia is on the other side of the mountain for safe keeping. We keep all our unit's munitions, including the C4 charges, fuses, and timers in a secure place. Are you familiar with this item?"

"Yes I used them last year on an operation I was on in Texas and Mexico, C4 is destructive stuff to play with you know."

"Khara, maybe tonight, when we are in bed again you can quietly fill me in. I'd like to know more about you."

"Sure no problem I'll be happy to tell you."

The Russians walk over to the young man to say hello during the meal, and he made the introductions. The four men all wore beards, khaki colored clothes, and they all had Islamic sounding names. The women were introduced as Gretchen Popovich, and her aid.

Khara and Olga observed them but did not do anything except continue to eat their meal. Olga spoke in Russian to Gretchen and asked her where in Russia she is from. The answer came back Chechnya.

Popovich is barely five feet tall with brunette hair and brown eyes. The aid was about six inches taller, with dark black hair and fiery light blue eyes almost like a wolf's eye. In a split second both Olga and Khara realize the aid is Gretchen and not the one identified as Popovich. Khara could not believe her luck. This time she is now face to face with the real terrorist of Time Square.

The thought of withdrawing her weapon and shooting her did cross her mind, but she realized this is not the most opportune time to kill Popovich. Too many armed men walking around in front of and behind her. Plus she is out in the open on top of a mountain with no escape route, or enough firepower to succeed and live to tell about it. The Russians say goodbye and walk down a dirt trail to their tents.

Finished eating the three of them saunter down a path to the other side of the mountain crest to the mouth of a small man-made cave. Two guards are sitting in front of the opening with automatic weapons lying on their laps while they smoke something other than a cigarette.

Khara is not impressed with the security arrangement she witnesses. She thinks to herself they will come back here at some point to take what she feels she needs to finish off Gretchen.

The storage cave is not too deeply dug into the side of the mountain. Stacked inside are boxes of explosives and ammunition lying on the floor in a haphazard manner. Upon seeing this Khara perceives their keeping of a written inventory is probably nonexistent. If she takes what she wants nobody will ever know it is missing.

After a quick inspection, Khara and Olga are left to walk around the camp by themselves as their escort is called away for some problem to be solved. With the supply cave behind them, they take the first trail they find, and it circles the entire encampment around the top of the mountain. Khara tries to make a mental map to take note of the different trails leading downward and keeps walking until she returns to where the two guards are sitting. One is fast asleep while the other is listening with earphones plugged into his mobile phone.

"You know Olga we can come back later to grab a few things and finish off Gretchen and her crew tonight."

"Funny I was thinking the same thing. The aid is the real Popovich. I remember the description I was given, but it will not matter because both of them will die."

"Yes, I agree we will kill them all before sunrise."

"Sounds like a valid plan to me Khara. It will be dark before we leave to go back to town to bring our clothes with us. The plan is we'll approach the two guards by the cave and with our knives finish them both off in silence before they realize what is happening."

***

About dinner time the triangle rings out, and everyone comes to the dining area for the last meal of the day. Some take their plates and sit on the ground around numerous small campfires, while others are at the tables scattered around. The time of day is dusk, and the sun is going down in the west of the Rocky Mountains.

The food tonight is barbecued brisket slow roasted with mesquite baked beans and coleslaw. Freshly baked rolls or cornbread is available to go with dinner. Khara grabs a pitcher of beer and brings it to the table. They begin to eat when Gretchen and her aid come up to the table and ask if they can sit with them. In Russian, Olga invites them to join them at the table.

"Thank you. My assistant has a rough time with English so I appreciate your speaking in Russian to me so she can understand."

"Not a problem, I will speak in Russian to both of you, besides I thought everyone in Russia also speaks English?"

"Both of us are from Chechnya, and my aid refuses to talk in Russian if she can help it; the language of the occupiers, but her English is not too fluent either."

Olga turns to Khara and translates what was said by the aid.

Khara whispers in her ear "bullshit she understands every freaking word we say."

Olga smiles and turns back to the fake Pupovich ignoring the aid.

"So I don't understand what your rebel group has in common with the POC?"

"The two groups have more in common than you think. Both of us want to bring our country back from the overseers, and we started to work together this year developing new weapons."

Continuing the conversation Olga tries to trick her to divulge information about what they are doing, although she has an idea already.

"What kind of new weapons are you working on?"

"Something the American government kept hidden for years, and we stole the undeveloped weapon from their secluded laboratory. Patriots are people who are willing to die for their country's liberty, and will sacrifice their lives if needed."

The fake Popovich now questions Olga as to why she is here, and what experience does she have in combat?

"When I was younger I was a member of the Russian Army, and they recruited me for the KGB. I traveled all over the world as an assassin for the Kremlin. My favorite post was in Cuba helping Castro and living in the best villas on the island. The KGB worked mainly in Havana where I made a lot of contacts which I still maintain to this day. Many times they come in handy. Now I am an American citizen, and want to help the POC retake the country."

The aid to Popovich heard what is said and her demeanor changes. The woman stands to leave stating she doesn't feel well. The two rebels excuse themselves and walk away from the table whispering to each other.

Khara, not speaking Russian, continues to eat the brisket.

Olga turns to Khara and translates for her what she said to the Chechens.

"The real Gretchen freaked, I saw her face when you said you were an assassin for the KGB. Time is fleeting, and we can't wait. Tonight we need to do this. Later the driver is taking us back to the hotel to grab our clothes, and before we go we need to set things up. Let's go back to the supply cave now. In a minute or two it will be dark out, and we will need only moonlight to guide us."

Finished eating so as not to arouse suspicion Khara flips her backpack on and takes her plate to the garbage area to empty the scraps. Afterwards, the two walk off on a trail heading past the transportation depot to the supply cave. Khara senses someone is following them, but it is dark, and although she turns her head a few times looking back she doesn't spot anyone.

In a whisper, she turns to Olga and tells her she thinks someone is behind them. They turn a corner on the trail as Khara steps aside into the brush, and stands in silence behind a tree listening for footsteps while withdrawing the knife from its sheath in her boot.

A few seconds later two of the bearded rebels come trotting down the trail obviously following them. Olga stops walking and takes a few steps backstopping before a curve in the path. The two men approach the turn when Khara jumps out behind them, grabs one by his thick hair and yanks his head back exposing his neck to her sharp blade. A jab and twist from her muscular forearm and wrist bring this victim to his knees drowning in his own blood.

The second man is startled and turns towards Khara while swinging around from his shoulder an automatic rifle. Olga is now within striking distance of him. She lunges onto his back wrapping her legs around his waist and grabbing him by the neck for support while she is plunging the point of her blade into his breast. The sturdy knife is burrowing in between his ribs and is thrashing about the chest cavity trying to pierce his heart.

Both men are now lying on the ground as the two of them wipe their blades clean on the dead men's slacks. Both of them place the knives back in their sheath as they drag the bodies off the path, into the underbrush, and continue on to the supply cave.

About to leave the trail, and come into a small clearing by the munitions cave Olga lifts her skirt up, grabs her Glock and screws on a sound suppressor after removing it from a Velcro attachment on her holster. With the gun at her side in the moonlight visibility is not the best so the two approach the guards head-on. One is on the ground leaning against the cave wall sleeping while the other is sitting, and playing games on his cell phone.

In a practiced movement, Olga raises her arm and fires twice into the chest of the guard playing on his phone with only a whisper of two popping sounds emanating from the weapon. The phone drops to the ground, and they enter the cave. They walk inside and Olga dispatches the other man who is fast asleep with two shots to the side of his head.

A quick tap on her phone and the flashlight enables Khara to grab some C4, fuses, a handful of timers and shoves them in her backpack. To make space she took out her MP7 and slung the strap over her shoulder. Olga took a loaded rifle, a few extra magazines, and also placed it around her shoulder. Both of them grabbed a few RPG's and put them in one of the dead guard's jackets which are found lying next to his body on the floor tying the arms together to make a sack.

"Okay, Olga we're done here. Let's go make some noise."

The two head back using the trail which goes all around the encampment they were on earlier, and head for Pupovich's tent. They approach the barrack from the rear as Khara sets the fuse and timer for ten minutes on some C4 and slips it under the base of the lower wooden structure. Before leaving she also places three more, and times them for ten minutes before going off.

Now they walk over to the vehicle staging area, open three hatches to different SUV's, and place a charge securely under the seats of each one. The doors to the vehicles are closed when they are done, and they try to find the young driver and call out to him.

"Hey it's getting late, and we need to go back to the hotel for our clothes."

The young man is with a dozen or so armed men when he calls out to them to wait a minute for him. The group of militia starts to walk towards the two when they appear to lower their weapons from their shoulders, and almost point them at the two women.

"Olga, Popovich must have warned them you are KGB, and you are probably here to kill her. Gretchen put two and two together is what I think."

With the men closing in Khara swings her MP7 around, and starts to fire at them. Olga also lowers her rifle and begins to shoot at the group. She is a marksman and her shots find their targets as some of the men who didn't reach cover soon enough are on the ground either mortally wounded or dead.

"Come on Olga jump in the back of this pickup truck, and try to hold on to something. I'll drive. We're going down the mountain."

A firefight begins, but the militia is pinned down for the moment as Olga is braced in the rear by the tailgate shooting at anyone who dares to raise their head. This allows the pickup to head for a dirt trail down a steep slope. Confused since the militia made a few trails on the mountain Khara decides to try the one directly ahead of where the truck is parked. The vehicle starts on its downward journey as the C4 they planted in various places explodes in the motor depot vehicles, and under the Chechen rebel's tent.

The flames from the explosions light up the night sky acting as a backdrop for Olga as some of the militia is able to hop in a few of the remaining SUV's which are parked some distance from the rest. The militiamen gun the engines and fly helter-skelter down the side of the mountain on the bumpy dirt trail chasing the two women. The pickup Khara is driving makes a sharp turn to the right and Olga slides to the side of the pickup's rear bed while trying to load an RPG. A straight vertical slope comes up quickly and she is thrown into the back of the truck and tries to brace herself somewhat. Aiming at the closest SUV following them she squeezes the trigger. Hearing the whoosh of the RPG Khara eyeballs the rearview mirror as the militia in the first chase vehicle lifts off the road when the explosion occurs. The vehicle rolls over to on its side slamming into a massive tree and bursting into flames.

The remaining militia begins to fire at them as the trail becomes almost a vertical drop. Khara again glances in the inside mirror, and the vehicles following them appear to slow down and stop. Shifting down into second she remembers the Rockies in some places shoot straight up and on the side of the roads are sheer cliffs all over the place. Slowing down considerably she opens her door and hangs out tapping Olga on the shoulder. Khara jumps off first and Olga slides off the rear gate after her onto the dirt trail as the pickup truck leaves them in the dust of its truck's wheels. Holding their weapons in their hands they release them before they hit the gravel path. Both tuck and roll to the rough brush on the trail's side hoping not to slam into a tree. A few seconds later their stolen truck drives off a cliff, falls down into a valley hundreds of feet below bursting into towering flames, and explodes on the jagged rocks.

Battered and bruised they slide over to the side of the road after retrieving their weapons, and start to crawl on their stomachs back up the mountain staying in the brush with their rifles in their hands. The militia empties out of their vehicles, and with high-powered flashlights start to search the area for their bodies. Apparently, the gunmen are not sure if both of the women escaped, or went over the cliff. But they are not taking any chances. By now they must know the two are dangerous.

The lights are coming slowly down the dirt trail looking for them. Olga whispers to Khara to roll over to the side about twenty feet away and a few feet higher up the steep incline.

The men are on each side of the path with Khara to the right of them and Olga lying below. Khara starts to shoot at the militia from the side hitting a few. The rest of the men turn to return fire at the spot where her muzzle flashes came from. Khara rolls down the cliff a few feet from where she fired after taking her shots. The nonmilitary trained militia men start to aim at where she fired a few seconds before now giving Olga targets to aim at, and they begin to fall in rapid succession. The remaining few men who are not wounded drop their weapons, and start to run back up the hill to the encampment to call for some backup help.

Olga and Khara meet on the road and pick up some of the choice guns and ammunition the men left as they ran away. Olga finds a few of the RPG's she chucked out of the pickup before it went over the cliff, and picks them up. Loading one in the front of her rifle she easily slung it over her shoulder, and both women headed back up the mountain trail. With the realization, they are left with no choice but to re-enter the camp and kill everyone off, or they will not be able to escape.

***

The fires on the crest of the mountain are illuminating the night sky enabling Khara and Olga to detect where they are going. The walk back is slow and they will be lucky if they don't step on a rattlesnake in the dark, but the two keep heading upwards ready to defend themselves at a moment's notice.

It is not too long before they are at the first encircling trail of the encampment, and are able to view the vehicles and tents aflame. Khara figured the explosions sent embers to the camouflage netting, and when they caught on fire the trees also lit up. As they enter the training compound with their weapons drawn they find nobody is around. The place is empty. All the trucks and cars are gone except for the burning ones. Walking over to another trail which appears to go down the slope she spots a convoy of red tail lights winding down the side of the mountain.

Olga realizes the flames are beginning to spread to all the trees and underbrush on the mountain.

"Khara we must drive off this mountain quickly before we are trapped up here. This is going to be a major forest fire, and we are going to be toast soon if we don't leave now."

To their chagrin, no cars or trucks remain here which are not on fire. Khara finds lying on the ground near the side of a dirt trail going downhill a Victory Hammer-S motorcycle. "Someone must have left it here in their hurry to escape the inferno, or it belongs to one of their dead militiamen. Come jump on behind me."

With their rifles slung over their shoulders, they run over to the bike, both struggle to pick it up, and right it.

"When did you learn to ride a motorcycle Khara?"

"Hop on before we are burnt alive, and I'll tell you later when we are safe, and off this mountain."

A wall of flames seventy feet high is rising all around them as the magnificent treetops of the forest burst into wooden candles as on a cake. Turning the ignition key she starts the V-Twin engine and shifts up to second gear. Olga hikes her skirt up and sits on it while wrapping her arms around Khara's waist holding on for dear life.

Revving the motor Khara starts on the winding downward spiral trying to keep ahead of the raging fire. They feel the immense heat emanating from behind as they ride and bump over the ruts in the dirt trail. The powerful headlight enables Khara to attempt to keep on the flat part of the path down, and not flip the bike over.

About two hundred feet ahead Olga discerns a checkpoint. Standing in the middle of the rutted trail are two armed men who must have been left in the rush to ride off the mountain and escape the flames. The two guards scrutinize the motorcycle coming down the path, and they raise their arms signaling for them to stop. Olga holds on to Khara with one hand and reaches down to her exposed thigh to lift out her Glock. Without waiting she starts to shoot at the men hitting both squarely in the chest allowing the motorcycle to pass uninterrupted on its way to the bottom of the mountain.

The Rocky Mountains are tall, and the roads all twist and turn in a circle rising up to the zenith of the peak. Every road is winding, and it is a rare find if one is straight up or down. All the passable pathways go in circles for the most part with few exceptions.

With her hands on the gas and clutch, she views scattered lights going horizontally below her in the valley. The lights tell her a normal paved street is ahead, and the bottom of the mountain.

Chapter Eight

The crisp mountain air is blowing in their faces as they are heading west on the paved state road. Khara is now driving back towards the town's few street lights glowing brightly in the dark valley below. The intensity of the raging forest fire on the mountain behind them is lighting up the asphalt. A rainless dry season makes it easier for the now massive inferno to feed itself as it is jumping from tree to tree, and spreading to the neighboring mountains.

The rumbling of the twin-V engine between her legs stirs her feeling of power as Khara steers the motorcycle down the curving Colorado road into the beginning of the town. Sirens are going off blaring, and people are running out of their homes onto the street to watch the nearby mountains belch its flaming fury into the night sky.

There are only two fire trucks located in the town. Their garage doors swing open as the emergency vehicles roar out racing to the flames with sirens screaming out into quiet of the nighttime valley air. Overhead Khara first hears then sees a searchlight beaming down from a prop plane flying towards the blaze. Men are leaving their homes carrying shovels and jumping in their car to race to the mountain to try to stop the forest fire from spreading.

The Victory motorcycle stops in front of the hotel, and they hop off to go inside. Don is behind the registration desk while the lobby is empty of others. He looks up and is shocked when both of them walk in and are in rough shape with bruises on their arms, dirt marks and grass stains are all over their disheveled and slightly torn clothes.

"What did you two do? The whole damn mountain range is up in flames, and you pop in on a motorcycle which obviously is not yours looking like shit."

"First I need to take a shower and afterward we'll come downstairs and explain everything to you. Also, I want to change my room to the one across from the one I am in now before I go upstairs."

"Why Khara the room was not comfortable for you?"

"No Don it is great, but I don't want to stay in the same room tonight. Believe me, I have my reasons."

The fact she carnally slept with the young leader of the militia in her bed last night causes her some concern. He knows what room she is in, and if he decides to revisit with a few of his men she wants to catch them from behind by surprise.

The women walk up to the second level, and Khara moves her stuff, which is not a lot, across the way to a room facing Main Street. Khara lifts her backpack onto the bed and her MP7. The door to her room opens and she gives the MP7 to Olga asking her to stand guard while she showers in the only bathroom on the floor down the hall. Not planning to stay in a room with no facilities she did not bring a bathrobe. With her coconut body wash in her left hand, and a towel over it she walks down the hallway naked to shower with her Sig Sauer in her other hand.

Finished she comes out of the bathroom and Olga enters and takes her shower. Meanwhile, Khara stands guard at the top of the staircase ready for unwelcome visitors wearing only a blue terrycloth towel around her waist and her MP7 at her hip.

The showers are over and done when they enter their rooms to change clothes and try to take a quick nap by setting their phone alarms for thirty minutes. After the alarm goes off they come back down for breakfast. There is no time for sleep as what is left of the militia escaped, and they have to get back to New York. There is not much here to do anymore.

In the lobby, Khara observes a lady behind the registration desk when she comes down the stairs, and calls out to her.

"Hey, where is the guy who stood here a little while ago?"

"He left. Said he received a phone call calling him back to his sick wife in New York. Why did he owe you money or something?"

"Nope I'm curious, no problem, and we'll be checking out after breakfast."

The small cafe is humming as they walk in and notices, sitting at a few tables are some locals getting coffee and eggs early in the morning before the roosters wake up. The sun hasn't come up yet but is about to rise, and the men in the restaurant are all talking about the forest fire raging on the mountain.

Both of them take a table in the rear of the room by a corner with both of them sitting with backs to the wall somewhat relaxed. In front of the cafe is a picturesque window facing the street, and trucks filled with men are driving through town heading to the conflagration. Until Khara views three black SUV's loaded with men park head-on by the hotel entrance, and men carrying automatic weapons exit.

"Olga I think we are going to have company for breakfast, the militia pulled up and parked and I think they are coming in here."

"Not to worry I am ready."

With her right hand she reaches down, and Olga lifts her skirt, placing her Glock on her lap while sliding the chamber back and cocking the gun. Next, she opens her pocketbook, takes out a loaded clip, and slides it under her left thigh. Now she is braced for action.

Khara reaches around, swings her pocketbook on the top of the table, and takes out her hand grenade placing it under two white polyester cloth napkins lying on by her place setting. She withdraws her Sig Sauer from her shoulder holster and she too places it on her lap pulling the linen tablecloth over it while cocking the firing pin. The waitress, a young local teenager, approaches her table and pours fresh brewed black coffee in their ceramic cups.

"What'll youse be eating this morning ladies?"

The girl takes Olga's order of a fried egg with cheese on a Kaiser roll while Khara continues to stare out the window, and mumbles something which sounds like a buttered freshly baked onion roll to the young girl.

"Okay give me a minute, and your food will be out soon."

Five men in camouflage fatigues enter the lobby as Khara shifts her gaze from the street, and beams in on the front door as they walk in the entrance.

"Whose motorcycle is parked outside the hotel?"

Khara hears one of them yell this out and is ready for trouble. Her senses heightened due to her being an Adrenalin junkie she answers him in a way to ensure he comes to her.

"Hey, asshole I drove it here, why?"

The four men walk into the restaurant area and stand by the entrance. One of them waves to someone hidden behind them. The leader walks out from behind them, and over to Khara's table. Now standing in front of his men he does not move. He is standing right in front of their table as Khara motions for the young man to sit down opposite her. He remains upright.

"Did you miss coming to my room last night, honey?"

With a puzzled expression on his face, he looks down at both of them.

"Okay Khara, before we kill both of you I want to know who the hell are you two?"

The other people in the room stand, and hustle out the rear door when they hear him speak to her leaving only the militia, and the two women alone in the restaurant. Without blinking, and looking at his eyes she starts to talk.

"Before anyone gets killed today I want to tell you how pleased I am for spending the other evening in my bed with you. The best thing I can say is you possessed stamina."

A sly smile crosses his face. "Thank you, but I'm still going to kill both of you in a few minutes."

"No, you're not. Olga is a former KGB assassin, and I am a detective with the New York City Police Department. In the past, I worked undercover with a lot of gang bangers all over this country. I've killed more drug dealing assholes than you can count on your fingers and toes."

After saying her piece Khara reaches under the napkin and pulls out the pin from the grenade exposing it for all to see.

"You can't run fast enough to escape the blast from this when it goes off. The fragments will travel over fifty feet a second. Think about this if you shoot me I let go, and you all die. This I guess is what you would call a Mexican standoff."

Faced with inevitable death he stares at her finger with the pin dangling in the air and starts to back off heading for the door.

"You are a beautiful son of a bitch Khara, and I'm not finished with you yet."

The men back out to the lobby as she and Olga raise their weapons ensuring the men don't try anything until they walk through the front door to the street. The pin is slipped back in while holding the grenade in her other hand. Satisfied it is restored she drops the grenade back in her pocketbook, and zippers it shut. Without saying a word both women drop to the floor and scurry on their hands and knees through the kitchen door where the young waitress entered only moments before.

Almost in the kitchen doors when multiple gunshots blast through the dining area's picture window punctuating the walls and doors in the room. Khara and Olga run out the side door by the hot stove and rush around to the front of the hotel through a small alleyway leading to the street. The asphalt is only a few yards ahead as they enter on Main Street, and see the armed men shooting into the building. The militiamen are about forty feet away from them, and to the side.

The two women stand shoulder to shoulder as they raise their arms to aim, and start to shoot at the militia. In an instant three of the men fall to the ground wounded as the other two, and the young leader run for protection behind their SUV's to return fire.

From the other side of the SUV's where the men are hiding more shots are fired, but they are not aimed at Khara. Don is coming at them from the other side of the street.

Only the young leader is left alive.

"Stop shooting I give up" he shouts.

Don yells out the standard command to the shooter not knowing who the guy is or why he has fired his gun.

"Throw down your weapon, and raise your hands above your head."

The man drops his pistol on the asphalt, and due to the distance from him, Khara does not notice the hammer is cocked. The gun goes off and the bullet strikes the building not harming anyone.

"Down on your knees, now!"

Don runs up to him, grabs his wrists, and places him in handcuffs. The lone police car in the town is notified and is coming back from the forest fire to secure the prisoner. Khara walks up to him and kisses him on the lips.

"The lady behind the registration desk is full of shit, and I knew it when she said to me you went back to New York to your sick wife. Why did you tell her misleading information, Don?"

"There are plenty of reasons. First I believed you would know she is lying, second you two had to be the cause of the forest fire when I saw you all roughed up and wearing torn clothes. The third reason is the motorcycle you girls rode into town on last night. The bike is not yours, and I put two and two together. Last night I figured someone will come looking for it; especially when you asked me to change your room to one right across the hall from it. So I waited patiently across the street in my rented car to help in case you might cause some kind of calamity, which you did."

"Well, we appreciate your assistance although we could have killed him if you didn't interfere."

"The guy is worth more to us alive. The bureau is sending their Denver agents out here to take him back. Last night I called them when you walked in the lobby. The FBI should be here in a minute or two, and

I'll need to go back with them to fill out a lot of reports."

"Oh, I never introduced you to my landlord. Olga Levinsky this is Don Weber, my fiancé."

Olga shakes his hand and smiles. Khara gives him another kiss and turns to leave.

"Bye Don we are going to head out to the airport now, and try to catch a flight back to the city. I'll see you in New York soon."

Khara leaves the expensive motorcycle in front of the hotel with the key in the ignition and starts to walk around to the rear parking lot where she left her rental car when she stops, and turns to the young man in handcuffs.

"Where are Popovich and her aid?"

"The two women are dead. The explosions you caused blew up her tent along with our vehicles. And I never saw them after you two escaped from the mountain base camp."

She heard what he said, and Olga starts to walk to the parking lot entrance.

"Sorry but I don't believe him, Olga."

"Why not he said she died in the explosion from the C4 charge we left under her tent?"

"Before we were to go to Russia two CIA agents visited me in Brighton. The three of us walked across the avenue to the boardwalk, and they said something to me which at first didn't make sense at first, but I understand the code now."

"What did they tell you?"

"The one agent told me dead girls don't die. Until I see her body in a casket I can't believe she is finished off."

"Well, we can't go back to the encampment Khara to make certain she died in the inferno. Everything in the base camp is burnt to a crisp. Nobody could survive the raging fire we caused. We'll need to assume she is deceased and gone for good."

"Maybe, come on let's leave the area. We did enough damage to this part of the Rockies."

As they approach the rental car Khara stops and turns to Olga. "Hey, I think I'll ride the motorcycle back to the airport. The short trip down the mountain reminded me of how much I enjoyed riding. See you back in Denver."

***

The trip back to the airport went smoothly. They checked in at the airline office with their diplomatic passports, and are cleared to fly. Both take their items and walk to the boarding gate where they will sit and wait for their plane to land. There is over an hour to kill with nothing to do. After they walked in the terminal Khara purchased two tickets back to New York on the next plane. The only seats available are in first class on the next airplane out of Denver to Newark Liberty. With time to waste each takes a turn napping while the other person keeps an eye out for anything which might look suspicious. The two women are pros and are smart enough not to let their guard down.

After a while, more people sit in the boarding gate area until it is almost full. Khara turned to Olga and said she will be back in a little while. She wants to purchase a water bottle at the newsstand a little ways back in the terminal. With enough time to spare she starts walking when she passes another boarding gate and views a woman sitting by a gate too well-dressed, hair and makeup done nicely, with a man in a suit next to her talking she thought to belong sitting in the airport. They looked out of place to her.

For a second she did not recognize the woman and stopped to take a second look. Engrossed in conversation with the man's back facing her the woman did not realize Khara is focusing in and trying to place the face.

Stepping a little further away from them she calls Olga to "come to gate fourteen, and hurry."

Olga approaches the gate area, and Khara tells her the well-dressed woman sitting over by the entry door is the fake Popovich.

"Are you sure Khara, we only met them once close-up?"

"There is only one way for us to find out. Let's go sit near her, and see what happens."

The two women calmly walk over and find empty seats opposite from the couple. Once they sit Khara looks over at them, and the woman's face freezes in astonishment.

Khara flips her gold detectives shield on a chain out of her blouse and stares into her face. Slowly she pulls her leather jacket back exposing her firearm.

"Don't you move or say anything if you want to live. Where is your aid?"

The well-dressed man sitting next to Popovich turns to Khara, and in a thick foreign accent tells her in broken English to screw off. Upon hearing what he said Olga, in Russian, warns him if he wants to live to walk on the arriving plane to shut up and sit still. A heated conversation in Russian begins between them, and he reaches into Pupovich's carry-on bag and starts to pull out a handgun.

Two shot ring out in the boarding area, and the well-dressed man falls back in his seat with his head slumped on his chest. The Chechnya rebel did not realize when Khara put her hand in her jacket pocket she is holding the small snub nose .38 pistol she bought recently in Virginia. For years she always carries a spare gun on her for security reasons. The few passengers in the area start to run away yelling for the police.

The fake Popovich starts screaming at the top of her lungs. Leaping across the small aisle with a left hook Olga slams her in the face splitting her lip causing blood to flow on her clothes, and knocking the woman off her seat to the floor. Khara bends over, grabs the woman by a handful of hair and the front of her blouse bringing the fake Popovich to a standing position. With each holding her under an arm they force the woman to walk with them to the family restroom situated only a few feet across from her gate area. Once securely inside with the door locked Khara starts to question her.

"Who are you, and where is the virus?"

"My name is Gretchen Popovich, I don't know what you are talking about, and who are you?"

"Listen bitch I am your worst nightmare. Where is your aid, and how did you escape alive from the explosions."

The woman ignores her threats, and she repeats a programmed answer.

"Look at my passport I am Gretchen Popovich. In case you cannot read English I have diplomatic immunity, and you can't hold me here. It's in my pocketbook, look for yourself, and I don't know what virus you are talking about."

Khara is pissed and places her right hand on the woman's shoulder, and presses in on a nerve. Wincing in discomfort the fake Pupovich falls to her knees.

Opening the woman's travel bag Olga takes out a Russian passport and shows it to Khara while reading it to her.

"In Russian, it says she is Popovich."

"Bullshit I already saw two of them die. Her passport is a forgery. Before I inflict more pain I want you to tell me how did you escape off the mountain?"

"My aid and I went in the forest relieving ourselves when we saw you kill two of our men by the supply cave. We believed you two must be professional killers and are either here for the militia or us. So we rushed back, and with two of our men grabbed our go bags, and jumped in our car to drive down the trail to escape before the explosions and fire. When we came to the highway we heard explosions behind us, and assumed you two to be responsible."

"And where is the real Popovich?"

"For the last time, I am Popovich, arrest me."

"Screw you bitch, you're starting to piss me off real bad. Tell me where I can find her and the virus."

Suddenly the woman pulls her hand out of her jacket pocket and pops a capsule into her mouth.

"My family will live in a free Chechnya, and I am prepared to die for them."

With no hesitation, and with all her strength, Khara punches her in the stomach hoping the violent force of the strike will cause her to spit the pill out. Unfortunately, she gulped and swallowed the pill. The woman falls to the tile floor convulsing as white foam begins to bubble up, and drools out of her mouth.

"Son of a bitch this is the second time this happened to me with Popovich. Next time I meet one of them I am taking all clothing off her, I don't care where we are situated. Look in her pocketbook and see if you can find any clues as to where her so-called aid is heading."

Olga searches through a bunch of papers in Russian when she opens a receipt for four airline tickets. Two are on a different airline than the one the fake Popovich is on. Two are for a flight to New York.

"Look this must be the place where the aid is flying to make her way back home. According to this we only have ten minutes to hustle to the gate before she flies off."

Khara drags the body away from the door and leaves her crumpled in a fetal position near the toilet. Olga opens the door to the room while pushing the button in to lock the door, and when Khara steps out they close it leaving the dead woman's body secure inside the family restroom.

Hustling they head for the gate where the aid is supposed to be waiting to embark. The airline representative is closing the boarding ramp door as they approach the loading area. The Popovich aid is already on the plane.

Khara runs up to the gate attendant as she almost closes the door completely.

"Stop I am a New York City detective and I believe the terrorist who killed thousands of people in Times Square is on this plane. It can't be allowed to take off."

The representative spots the gold detective's shield dangling from her neck.

"Are you sure it is not easy to delay a flight."

"You need to hold it here and check the names of the passengers on the plane. Is a Popovich on it? We have our terrorist cornered if she is on the plane."

The airplane starts its engines but has not left the gate yet. The woman walks to the podium and begins to scroll down the list of the passenger's names.

"Yes, a Popovich is flying on the flight to New York. She is traveling with a companion. The two are seated in the middle of the plane. I'll call security and halt the takeoff. In a minute there will be police and some federal air marshals here also."

After making the call the plane's engines start to turn off. The representative turns to Khara to explain what the pilot is going to do.

"Now he is going to make an announcement the flight is delayed at the terminal for technical issues, and he hopes to take off once the mechanical problem is fixed. Soon the police will arrive and I will notify the pilot to ask the passengers to disembark to supposedly take another flight."

The air marshals arrive first, and all passengers are asked to leave the plane. The people walk off the boarding ramp and they are requested to show their tickets and identification. Everything is going smoothly until a strikingly beautiful tall redheaded young girl in a tight fitting sweater with blue jeans, and her boyfriend walks off the plane identifying herself as Popovich.

Khara goes over to the woman and gets in her face.

"Who the hell are you?"

"Am I in trouble? My boyfriend and I are going to Las Vegas on a short flight on our school break. A foreign man and woman approached us in the terminal and asked if we would like to go to New York all expenses paid. Of course, I said yes, and she gave me her passport, boarding pass, and three thousand dollars in cash. The lady said in broken English to cover the picture in the passport with the ticket when I boarded the plane. I gave the woman my boarding passes to Las Vegas. The flight left about ten minutes ago and should land in a little while."

Turning to the representative Khara asked, "when is the next flight to Vegas today?"

"In one hour from another boarding gate. Here is the information you need. If you like I can purchase two tickets for you from my podium?"

"Okay let's do it."

Looking at the red-haired woman Khara asked where she is going to stay when she arrives in Las Vegas.

"We did not make any reservations before we left. No worry I am sure plenty of hotel rooms are available off the strip in Las Vegas. My friends always told me rooms are plentiful."

Talking to Olga Khara explains what she thinks is happening.

"Popovich is smart. She is not going to stay in Las Vegas. She will either book another flight out as soon as she arrives, or she will rent a car and drive somewhere. We still have a chance to catch her in the terminal if she is flying out. Depends on where she is going."

The airline representative is listening and says she can check to see if a Popovich on any of her airline's other flights out of Las Vegas. "The lady you are searching for might book a flight out while she is on the airplane with the stewardess."

"It's worth a try. Go ahead and check it out for us."

"Sorry but I don't see anyone with the name Popovich booking any flight with us from Las Vegas."

"Do you know if any international flights are going to Russia or Europe from Las Vegas?"

"Yes, but we transfer in Chicago where she can go with no layovers or stops to Iceland and transfer to a flight to Moscow. From our airline, this is the only way to do it."

"What time does the flight from Vegas arrive in Chicago, and the one we will take from Denver now?"

"The flight from Las Vegas will leave in three hours. Our flight to Chicago leaves in thirty minutes, but only first class seating is empty and available."

"Book us two seats, cancel the Vegas flight, and board us on the next one to Chicago. We'll meet her at the gate when she gets off to transfer, and here is my credit card."

The tickets are printed, the plane is told to wait for them, and Khara and Olga rush to the departing gate to board their flight to Chicago. "We are taking a big chance Khara the real Popovich will be on the flight to O'Hare airport in Chicago. Are you pretty sure about this?"

"It is a safe bet she'll be on it, I think. In all likelihood, she has the vial with the virus and the instructions on how to spread it as vapor. There is no reason for her to stay in the country anymore. Wait a minute for me I need to call Johanna now and tell her to inform Homeland Security to meet us in Chicago."

Khara walks to a window to be by herself and dials Johanna in New York on her private phone number.

"Johanna Khara, I tracked Popovich to Las Vegas, and I believe she will be flying to Chicago to switch to a Reykjavik Airlines flight to Iceland, and then on to Russia. It is important for you to send Homeland Security to Chicago to meet me at the airport. I can identify her to them. Also, I'll need a manifest of people on the Vegas plane who will be continuing their travels flying to Iceland on the airline about the time the Vegas flight lands."

"I'll call Homeland Security on it right away. Be careful I don't want to lose you to a deadly virus."

***

The flight to Chicago takes off and the two are seated in First class with free liquor offered to them. Khara asks for a beer, and Olga orders a shot of whiskey.

"So now we are on a plane, and we know there is some time left to kill. Tell me how you were taught to ride the motorcycle you stole."

Sitting back in the plush wide first-class leather seat she takes a sip of her ice cold beer and begins to explain to Olga how she learned to handle a motorcycle.

"Many years ago when I first started with the police department they assigned me to the narcotics division in Brooklyn doing undercover work. I believe I was chosen because being an unknown cop, black, and I spoke Spanish so the brass ordered me to hang out in dingy bars where a lot of minority drug dealing gangs meet. Also the fact I studied Krav Maga hand to hand combat for years played into their decision too. Since I am capable of defending myself they thought I would be a good fit to infiltrate a gang if I hung around with them long enough."

"So you are able to make your way into a drug gang?"

"It is not easy. I went around to a lot of dive bars in run-down neighborhoods at night trying to make contacts so I could purchase with police cash some stuff to resell. Whatever I bought I turned over to my sergeant who at the time is my supervisor in the department. For six months until I became a fixture on the scene I went to these bars and private clubs. The sellers would buy me drinks, and besides the money, I gave them they would expect some payback for helping me out in their business. So I enjoyed a few drug dealer boyfriends until I was accepted without question into their circles."

"So your drug dealing boyfriends are bikers too? Did the police know about your so-called friends?"

"The department is aware they existed. It is the old story of don't ask don't tell. So long as I didn't arrest them there is no entrapment, and my dates treated me okay considering they are ruthless when it comes to money or drugs. My big break happened in a bar and grill in Red Hook Brooklyn called The Flamingo Bar and Grill. This hangout only played loud Latin music all day and night. The drinks are strong, the food minimal, and it is dark. There are booths lining the sides and back walls with a few small tables in the middle. In the rear, they had a game room where there are two pool tables, a lot of gambling going on, and drug dealing. On weekends they brought in a few cheap Spanish or black hookers for their entertainment. "

"My divorce came through about a year after I was on the job so I had no problem dating a few of these guys. The truth is I really didn't care about my marriage, and if any of them acted frisky when I didn't want to play I put them in their place quickly. The whole bunch who hung out there knew not to screw with me after some huge asshole thought he could have sex with me when he decided he wanted some fun. It didn't occur to him I did not find him appealing. So when this giant lifted me up, pinned me against the wall, and tried to kiss my breasts I slapped my hands over his ears inflicting a lot of pain. He dropped me, and I kicked him in the groin. As he was holding himself on the floor I took out my knife and sliced off his left ear. I yelled at him in Spanish if he ever does that to me again it won't be his ear I cut off. After this incident, they all treated me differently, with respect."

"His buddies let you get away with cutting him?"

"Believe me if I had been one of their squeezes he would be dead before my feet ever touched the floor. The girls who hung around them are handed off to any of the guys who wanted one. Guess he thought I am one of the whores in the bar. The asshole learned I wasn't one of them. The truth is the men who are hanging in the place at the time started to laugh when he stood, and only had one ear. About a month later he overdosed on heroin. There is a guy in the rear watching this go down who I suspected to be a major drug dealer. He walked over to me and asked if I would like to go for a ride. At this moment I knew I am in their good graces. This would be the break I needed. I went outside with him, he drove a loaded Harley and parked it on the sidewalk. Not making a sound he motioned for me to jump on behind him, and he drove off with my arms around his waist."

"Where did he take you?"

"Mill Basin, on the water; the guy owned three homes in Canarsie right on the inlet. The three are side by side he told me. The garage door opened in the middle house and he pulled in and shut the door behind us. The first time I walked in the house with him he said I could stay in it if I would be his bitch. Bullshit I told him. I'm not owned by anyone, and if he wanted me to live in the house with him I wanted to know who is in the other homes on either side."

"He said it is none of my business. I know it sounds like I am picking a fight with him but these guys only respect strength. I came right back at him and said unless I know what is going on where I live I'm not going to stay here with him. I accused him of being a cop and trying to set me up. I wanted him to go on the defense, not me."

"So he told you about the houses on either side of you?"

"Yeah he gave me a bull shit answer but a week later I found out what is going on. The house on the right he stored his drugs in the basement, and he installed window shades in every room; lights tied to automatic on and off switches so it looked like people lived in it to not raise anybody's suspicions. The house on the left he actually stayed in. The middle house is where I started to live in and is the place where he partied and parked his bike so not to disturb the neighbors. Believe it or not, he wanted to be a considerate drug dealer so nobody would report his activities."

"What did he look like?"

"I thought he looked good, and he is tall, with tats all over his muscular body. I liked his mustache too, but I hated the beard. His blue eyes drove me crazy."

"On weekends he taught me how to ride with him, and when I was good at it he bought me my own Harley. Anything I needed he would give me money to buy, food, clothes, jewelry. The only thing is I couldn't arrest him because I slept with him, and it might cause the case to be thrown out of court. So I waited almost four months until I pretty much became knowledgeable about his schedule. One afternoon I called my supervisor from a payphone and told him when a shipment is coming into the storage house. My boyfriend is always present when the shit arrives to pay for the stuff and make sure it is not fake powder or some crap like it. The department waited, staked out the house. When they thought they collected the evidence they needed the strike force moved in, and arrested him for dealing drugs."

"So when he went to prison where did you live?"

"I continued to stay in the house for a while because he put the place in my undercover name, and he never found out my real name. My cover is not blown; to this day my fake ID and street cred is still valid if I need them. Also, my fake brokerage account is also making money for me. I retained a debit/credit card from them which I keep in case I need to bug out and disappear sometime in the future. No one in the department remembers I still possess it. My supervising sergeant from undercover work is dead because I killed him in self-defense. Later I transferred out of the narcotics squad, and somehow records which are tracking me were lost or misplaced by my new supervisor."

The pilot came on the intercom and announced they are cleared for landing in Chicago.

Chapter Nine

Anticipating how she is going to either capture or kill Pupovich Khara decides to lay out a plan with Olga before the airplane lands. First, she wants to ask the stewardess a quick question. The call button above her head is pressed, and a short while later a middle-aged woman in uniform approaches her seat.

"I understand a flight from Las Vegas will be arriving in Chicago an hour or so after we land. Can you try to find out for me which part of the terminal the plane will taxi to because I need to meet someone coming in on it?"

"Sure give me a second please, and I'll be right back."

Khara views her go forward and pick up a phone. It is not long until she returns and tells her the gate number. The stewardess explains the gate is in the same terminal the passengers on this plane will be disembarking.

Olga also listens to the answer and waits for the woman to walk away.

"What is your plan Khara to shoot her when she walks off the airplane? You know this is what I would do. In the confusion we can easily slip away unnoticed, I did this before in Bratislava Slovakia when I needed some chaos to escape."

"If I need to I will. Johanna will notify federal law enforcement, and they will be waiting at the gate for us. The lab guys will in all likelihood be in white hazmat suits carrying guns if the bureaucracy has its way. I do not think there is a way we can do what you suggest. Also, I would rather capture her alive this time to make points with Johanna, and the big brass."

"You think they may give you a medal or promotion?"

"Doubt it. I don't think I will become famous, but if I did I could run for political office. Wouldn't it be a scream if I won?"

"Yes, but who would ever elect someone who is a totally unqualified person?"

"Never know Olga. Stranger things happened in the past. After we land I'm thinking we wait by the side of the door to the ramp in the terminal since we are the only ones who can recognize her. She will, in all likelihood, be under an assumed name with a fake passport again. This time the so-called aide, and real Popovich, will be caught."

The flight arrives at O'Hare International Airport on time, and taxis to the terminal to discharge all the passengers. Khara and Olga are let off the plane first since they are the only ones in first class and enter the terminal. The walkways are packed with people shoulder to shoulder, and getting through the thousands of passengers is difficult. At last, they approach the gate where the airplane from Las Vegas is scheduled to arrive in two hours if it is on time.

To their surprise no men in white hazmat suits are present, but a lot of police, federal marshals, and FBI Special Agents to make the arrest. Khara walks up to a man who appears to be in command and shows him her identification.

"I am Detective Khara Bennet from New York City. Are you in charge of this detail?"

"Yes detective, the bureau is in control now, and we are going to set up a parameter around this gate to prevent people from entering the area. Washington informed me you would be here to assist in the capture of the terrorists."

"I know what she looks like, and I am here to identify her when she walks off the plane. What I suggest is we change the gate to one in an isolated walkway of the terminal. The information I gathered is she is traveling with a forged diplomatic passport, is armed, and with a male companion who is also considered dangerous. I believe both of them are suicidal if captured, or will fight to the death if cornered."

"Thank you for your input. I'll call the airport and switch the arriving gate. Not a bad idea. I think too many people are crammed in around here if something does go wrong."

"By the way, I asked my assistant commissioner to obtain a copy of the manifest of travelers on the incoming flight who will be continuing on with Reykjavik airlines to Iceland. This way we will know how many people are on the flight."

The FBI agent walks away and calls in the request to switch the landing gate. In a few minutes he comes back, and announces the plane from Las Vegas will be arriving at the last numbered gate located near the end of a long terminal.

"Detective Bennet the tower switched the arrival to Terminal One, Concourse B, and gate B 22. This is at the end of a long segregated wing of the airport. They will be closing the section for anyone who would normally use gates B 21 through B 24 for us. There are no other gates for people to walk to at the end of this terminal. I will order officers to be stationed at the entrance to this hallway to keep any early passengers for later flights out of harm's way."

"Fine, I like the plan so far. My partner and I will wait by the side of the ramp door so we can tell you which one she is. I can also describe her for you. She is about five foot five, maybe six, short jet black hair, baby blue eyes and speaks with a Russian accent in broken English. Do you have a female agent who can change into one of the airline agent's uniforms, and hold a clipboard while asking departing passengers their names to match against the manifest? This way if Popovich changes her clothes or hair color we can still catch her. I am sorry but I can't help you with the description of her male traveling companion. By the way how many women on the manifest are flying on to Iceland?"

"I was told three women will be going on to Reykjavik today from this flight. They are coming in on a larger intercontinental plane which will board additional passengers and continue on to Iceland and Russia."

"Tell your agent to hold a handkerchief in her hand as she checks off the women leaving the plane. If it is one of the three have her wipe her brow. Popovich is smart, and I don't trust her not to pull a fast one on us."

"Good idea Detective. I have four female agents assigned to this operation. It will be taken care of within the hour. We will segregate the men from the women going to Iceland so we can try to limit any more casualties than needed to capture her."

With time to kill Olga and Khara take a short stroll in the airport to grab a quick bite to eat for lunch. There is a branch of a famous Philadelphia restaurant open in the terminal, Love and Honey Fried Chicken, so they go in and sit down at a table. The food is fabulous, reasonable, and served up quickly. They order the fried chicken with a side of hush puppies and green apple slaw.

"Wow Khara this chicken is so moist, it's delicious. Glad we stopped in here."

"I know I'm so full otherwise I would order seconds. C'mon we need to be going. I want to make sure everything with the FBI is according to plan."
     ***

They are walking to the last gate at the far end of the terminal when they notice the hallway curves. No one can see in a straight line to the gates located at the rear of the wing if they were to walk down the corridor. This will help keep onlookers away, and safe if there is a violent outcome to this operation.

An FBI agent dressed in a gray nondescript suit walks over to where Khara and Olga are sitting, informs them the plane is cleared for landing and should be on the ground at the gate in about thirty minutes. There are agents dispersed and hidden on the tarmac below the terminal in case someone tries to jump off the airplane after it lands.

While they are walking Olga asks Khara a question.

"Hey, since there are a few minutes to spare tell me what is going on with the Mexicans who are trying to kill you? I heard about your shooting at the Verrazano Bridge toll plaza before we left for Colorado."

"When this is over I'm going to speak to Junior and find out what ideas he might be thinking up. He understands, as well as you, the Colonel from the Mexican Secret Police will not stop until he is either dead or succeeds in killing me and you guys."

"I think we want to make a trap for him. Let me see what Viktor has in mind when we arrive back to Brooklyn."

A loud whistle blows, and the FBI agent in charge orders his agents to be set in place. The plane is almost to the gate, and the agents keep an eye on the arrival as it is pulling near the terminal. The ramp is extended at a slow pace to the plane's door for the people to disembark, and enter the terminal. Khara and Olga go over to the loading area and position themselves on either side of the door behind the gate agent's desk.

As the passengers walk off the plane a female FBI agent dressed in the airline's uniform checks off each individual's name as they leave. The plan is when she wipes her brow with a handkerchief a federal agent walks up to the woman passenger as she enters the terminal hallway, and escorts her to the side of the walkway to stand by a wall. Khara and Olga examine each of them with intensity looking for a woman who fits the description to be pulled to the side. All the passengers are off, the FBI states one is missing, and not checked off the manifest. The female agent with the clipboard turns to Khara and says one woman is missing. Khara gives a quick look over to the three women, and none of them fit the description of Pupovich.

With her Sig Sauer in her hand, she slides the barrel back to cock the hammer, enters the ramp, and walks toward the plane. Olga, her is behind ready for action. The pilots and stewardesses grab their bags and walk past Khara as she runs on the plane.

First Khara glances into the cockpit, and it is empty. With a slight turn, she steps into the front galley and calls out into the cabin.

"Gretchen there is no escape. I'm coming for you. If you want to live, and see Chechnya become independent step out with your hands raised over your head."

Silence permeates the cabin. There is no response. Both walk to the back of the airplane inspecting each row of seats as they go. A gun in her hand she opens the restroom doors, and they too are empty. No sound is made as Khara points to a door at the rear of the plane, and they open it slowly. There are tiny steps leading upstairs to the crew's relaxation area. Olga points up and goes first. Both of them climb the steep stairs where it leads to a small windowless area with small cramped beds where the crew can sleep. In the far bed, Khara spots a woman sleeping. Olga goes over to her to wake the woman.

"Khara she's dead and is only in her bra and panties. This woman probably is a stewardess. We now know someone killed her and left the plane dressed as part of the flight crew."

"We need to run back quickly. With any luck the FBI kept everyone segregated."

Their guns put away they rush down the hatch to the cabin and run out the front door of the plane. Khara starts yelling for the FBI to hold all the passengers and crew. The agents only held the passengers. They let the flight stewardesses and pilots walk down the long hallway. Khara calls out to the agent in charge.

"Keep your eyes on them while we try to find the crew before they leave this wing. Popovich killed a stewardess, and took her identity."

Olga and Khara race after the teal uniforms walking away, and almost out of the terminal hallway where they are located, and yells out to them.

"Stop, stop where you are; police, don't move."

Everyone freezes except for one of the stewardesses. She walks a few steps more and turns to face Khara and Olga. With no words spoken, she reaches into her carry-on bag, pulls out an automatic pistol, and begins to shoot at them.

Khara and Olga split, and hide behind a large column on the sides of the walkway to protect them from Pupovich's bullets as they ricochet away. The flight crew starts to run by Popovich, and as one of the older stewardesses pass Gretchen she grabs her by the hair, wraps her left arm around the woman's neck, and points her pistol at her head. The middle-aged woman begs to be let go, but every time she says something the grip on her throat gets tighter. Her captor slips her hand over to her uniforms inside breast pocket and pulls out a test tube filled with a liquid.

Khara peers out from the column, and calls to Pupovich.

"Let her go there is no escape. You are done."

In broken English Gretchen answers her in a deep Russian accent.

"No, you are finished. Unless I walk on a plane going to Iceland before it leaves I will open the test tube, and everyone in O'Hare Airport will die. The virus will float in the air and multiply while flying down to the lobby of the terminal below us"

Believing the woman is not making a false statement, and she is to be considered suicidal, Khara cannot let thousands of innocent civilians be killed due to the virus escaping.

"Gretchen this is your last chance. At the count of three, I'm coming out to kill you."

The FBI task force hears this, is thirty feet or so behind her, and is watching the drama unfold helpless to do anything.

"One...."

"No stop, we will arrange your safe passage out of here" a voice beckons from behind Khara.

The federal agent in charge runs up to Khara, and orders her to "stand down detective; we can't chance her opening the vial. I asked agents to be hidden on the plane who volunteered for a possible suicide mission to take her prisoner once they are in flight over the ocean."

Khara stares at him in disbelief. "Are you out of your mind? We cornered her, and you are going to let her go, and chance escaping? She is a violent terrorist."

"We are faced with no choice detective. She can wipe out the whole airport in minutes."

"You're an asshole." Without saying anything further to the head agent Khara turns to face Popovich, and aims her pistol intent on ending the standoff.

A shot is fired, and the hostage and Popovich are both hit with the same bullet. It travels through the hostage and hits Popovich in the pelvic area knocking her over. They both fall to the floor with Popovich rolling to the left a few inches away from the hostage, and still holding the vial in her other hand. Once she is separated from the woman Olga and Khara run toward her opening fire hitting Pupovich numerous times as her body recoils up off the floor from every hit. The shooting stops and Popovich are motionless on the floor. The FBI agents run to each of the fallen women, and Olga grabs the unopened vial while Khara picks up Pupovich's pistol, secures it, and feels for a pulse on the two women's necks.

"Call an ambulance they both are still alive."

The agent in charge hustles over to Khara and takes Pupovich's gun and test tube from her for evidence. "Now we can't question Popovich if she dies detective."

"Screw you, and the FBI. I saved thousands of people from being killed if she escaped, or somehow crashed the plane in the city proper. It doesn't matter because she is not the woman I saw in Colorado."

The agent is speechless.

Face to face and looking the agent in the eye she reminds him one of the male passengers they are still holding down the hallway leaning against a wall is also a terrorist. The problem is which one.

"What do you think we should do detective, shoot them like her?"

"It would solve the problem, but you're too afraid some pussy in Washington might have a shit-fit."

The agent appears to Khara to be pissed at her for talking to him in such a manner. The agent in charge turns and walks back down the hallway to try to figure out who is the male terrorist they are holding with the other passengers.

Khara and Olga follow behind him as they approach the wing where all the male passengers are secured. The men are out of the sight line from the shooting and only heard the gunshots. An FBI agent walks over to his supervisor and informs him they have no way of telling who the bad guy is. Puzzled the lead agent stops and looks at Khara and Olga.

"Do you two have any idea how to identify the terrorist without killing him?"

"Yes, ask them to say their names out loud. If he speaks with a Russian accent pull him out of the line, and make him lay on the floor spread eagled keeping a gun aimed at the suspect all the time. You can always detain whoever you think it is for questioning later in a secured area. Also, keep your eyes on their hands. Don't let them reach into their pockets for anything. They all have poison pills and will commit suicide before being captured."

"It might work since we have no other way to find out. I'll ask them now."

Khara walks a few feet behind him as he approaches each male passenger one at a time, and asks him to state his name.

As the lead agent works his way through the men one man near the far end steps out from the line. He flips his hand to his mouth and swallows a pill before anyone can stop him.

"Free Chechnya" is the last words he says before falling to the floor.

The agent calls for a medic to help the fallen passenger.

Khara turns to the lead agent, and with disdain in her voice tells him off.

"Save your breath, he will be dead before you take another step. I've seen this before. I warned you to watch them a ...asshole."

"I had enough of your attitude detective. There will be a full report to Washington, and I will make sure to mention your uncooperative demeanor."

"Screw you, and the FBI. I'm going back home to Brooklyn. Go write whatever the hell you want in your damn report to daddy."

      ***

The flight back to Newark Liberty Airport is uneventful. Both of them are able to relax and fall asleep right away so they are not tired when they land in New Jersey.

There is a stretch black limousine waiting by the arrivals level. Viktor sent it for Olga to bring her home to Brooklyn. Khara takes out her phone as they left the plane and calls Johanna.

"Hey, Johanna I'm in Newark, want some company tonight for dinner?"

"Sure I would love to catch up with you. I heard what you did in Chicago, and the FBI are steaming mad. But the Homeland Secretary is cool with it because I spoke to him only a few minutes ago. I'll be home before you arrive at my place."

"See you soon, I won't belong."

Olga asks if she needs a lift to Caven Point in Jersey City where Johanna lives in a condo on the water.

"It would be great if you can Olga. I would appreciate it."

The driver opens the trunk, places their backpacks in, and he closes the rear passenger door once the two women are seated inside. The trip to Caven Point is not long, and soon Khara is dropped off by Johanna's building.

As Khara takes her bags from the trunk Johanna comes walking up to her after leaving the New York Water Ferry dock.

"Hey welcome back Khara. I heard all about the airport shooting, and I calmed the Secretary down. He was a little upset but I explained you must have had a good reason to piss off the lead FBI agent."

"He is an asshole. I didn't want to chance Popovich getting away, and maybe kill thousands of more people. She had to die."

"I understand your shooting the woman at O'Hare Airport, but Interpol informed us an hour ago a Gretchen Popovich is being followed as we speak. The woman registered into a hotel in Hamilton Bermuda. This Popovich went from Vegas to Atlanta and on to Bermuda. The police are lying back, and waiting to see who shows up at her hotel room."

"Son of a bitch Popovich had a double lead us on a wild goose chase to Chicago. Do you need me to go to Bermuda?"

"Not tonight Khara. Let the FBI or CIA do something useful. I have other plans for you this evening. Let's grab a bite to eat come on."

"Where do you want to go?"

"My condo, and I'll order food in for us."

They enter the living room and Khara places her bags on the floor, sits down on a counter stool in the kitchen, and is hungry.

"Where are you going to order from Johanna? The Italian place in uptown Bayonne is good. I enjoyed their food."

"Yes, they are a gourmet restaurant. What do you want to eat? Here is their menu."

"The whole menu sounds good; I'll have the sautéed chicken livers in a balsamic reduction with onions over a salad."

"Fine I'll order the same thing I've had it before, and it is delicious. Give me a minute to phone the order into them."

After dinner, they walk to the living room and sit on the sofa to watch the late news. The channel switches to their Chicago affiliate, and a reporter is at a press conference at O'Hare Airport. The FBI lead agent is at the microphone saying how the bureau stopped a terrorist from escaping with assistance from the Chicago Police Department.

"The son of a bitch never mentions us, Johanna. If it was up to him she would open the test tube on the plane as the flight took off over Chicago killing the crew, and crashing into the city. Thousands of more people could have been killed. These terrorists when cornered are all suicidal so you need to kill them when you can."

"Don't worry I'm going to put you in for a commendation. It's getting late and I have to wake up early tomorrow."

"Not a problem Johanna, Lets shower and we can go in together to Manhattan tomorrow. I need to see my shrink. Maybe, Eloise, she is out of the hospital by now. Did you ever pick up the coconut body wash I use?"

"Yes, and I also bought you a bottle of Chanel No.5 perfume; it's on the top shelf of the medicine cabinet."

***

Before leaving in the morning Khara calls Eloise and the service informs her she is still in recovery in a rehab unit of the hospital.

The ferry into lower Manhattan leaves them off on the east side near the Battery, and an unmarked police sedan is waiting for Johanna to bring her to One Police Plaza. The squad car reaches the City Hall area where they drop Khara off by the subway so she can take it uptown to the hospital to see Eloise.

The subway ride is not too long but it is rush hour, and the trains are packed tight with people going to work. Over her jacket, she is wearing her backpack with her MP7 in it as she wiggles between people until she can grab hold to a pole. The small suitcase she is wheeling contains the unassembled sniper rifle. The ride is going without incident for her until she reaches her stop. As she starts to exit the train through the mass of passengers she can feel a hand caress her rear end on the right side. Khara stops for a second as she is about to leave, looks at the pervert, raises her knee and strikes him in the groin area. Unfazed she continues walking out of the subway car onto the platform taking the stairs up to the street.

Since the hospital is only a few blocks away Khara starts to walk. As she approaches the Second Avenue entrance she flips her gold badge out of her blouse, waves it to security while walking in, and stands by the elevator without being stopped. The board on the wall tells her the rehabilitation unit is in the west wing on the fifth floor so she presses the button when she enters the elevator. The door opens, and she steps off into the rehab lobby. The nurse's station is right in front of her, and a nurse directs her to Eloise's room after Khara asks about her.

A few knocks on the door, and Khara enters noticing her sitting on a chair reading.

"Hey Eloise, how are you feeling today?"

"What a pleasant surprise, come over here and let me kiss you hello."

Khara goes over and Eloise kisses her on the lips as usual.

"Did the doctor say how long until you will be discharged from here?"

"I should be out in a day or two. I hired a nurse to help me at home for a few weeks. I need to get out more and do some walking. Care to stay with me for a few days and help out?"

"You know I can't stay in your apartment, and place you in danger if I am followed. I have to go to Mexico and deal with the Mexican Secret Police Colonel who is shipping in drugs to our country. Plus the terrorists are still out there. One is holed up in a hotel in Bermuda, and Interpol is watching her every move."

"So you didn't kill Popovich? I'm surprised you must be slipping."

"No, I killed her, or at least her double. So far three Pupovich's I know of died. One CIA agent wanted to use a code or phrase when I almost went to Russia to meet my contact. Listen to what he wanted me to use as a code, dead girls don't die."

"Those are strange code words Khara."

"Yeah I thought so too, but he explained it to me. Popovich is dead, yet she keeps popping up alive somewhere. The Chechnya rebel group under her is clever. The FSB is aware of her movements but have trouble tracking her travels. They have a mole deep undercover in her network and is trying to keep them apprised of her every move. But she is smart and so far has suicidal subordinates doing her work for her. To their knowledge, she wants to use the virus to kill Russians in their major cities. Her plan is when the Kremlin finds out it is a Persian Goat Virus only found in Iran they will start a war with the Ayatollahs. Iran will retaliate and destroy Moscow and weaken Russia. When it happens Chechnya can revolt, and declare its independence from Moscow. This is the crazy rebel's plan. They tested the virus out in New York with financial backing from the crazy right wing militia here in the states, especially out west. I know all about them because Johanna sent me there the other day."

"So you were the person who started the massive forest fire in Colorado this week Khara? It is on all the national news channels."

"I kind of sort of started it. I tried to kill off the terrorists by blowing them up with C4, but the trees caught on fire. Olga and I were lucky to escape with our lives."

"To be honest with you when I saw the reports of the fire on television, and I knew you were away on an assignment I kind of put two and two together. I'm relieved you're back in one piece. How about when I feel better we take another cruise together?"

"Sure I enjoyed our last one a lot, thank you. Book it when you feel better, and I'll go. Listen time is flying by and I need to go back to my place. How about I call you tomorrow?"

"I look forward to it Khara, love you."

With a quick kiss, Khara leaves the room and walks out of the hospital, and back to the subway. With noon fast approaching the rush hour congestion is finished, and she enjoys a quiet train ride back to Brooklyn.

Khara calls Junior while sitting on the train to ask him if he thought about what he is going to do concerning the Colonel.

"No Khara... I did not give the subject much thought. I am sure Victor and Olga will come up with something because they have the contacts with the Colonel through their Cuban sources, and he is more devious than I can ever be. In the meantime, I transferred Big Boy and his crew to assist me in the funeral home, and protect me at the same time."

"Good thinking Junior. I'll be back to you soon."

Thinking to herself about what he said she realizes Junior is not a heavyweight like his father. This time she will probably need to handle the Colonel with Olga's help.

At the DeKalb Avenue station, she transfers to the Brighton BMT line and continues to Brighton Beach. Walking down from the elevated station she senses, in a strange way, at home. It has been a long time since she felt this comfortable in a living situation. The smell of the salty ocean air is still invigorating as she crosses Brighton Beach Avenue, and heads to her apartment.

The doorman greets her with a front gold tooth smile as he opens the door for her to enter. In the lobby the concierge waves and hands over some mail he is holding for her until she returned.

Once back in her apartment she checks the security light and knows nobody has entered since she left. Placing her backpack in her bedroom she walks into the kitchen and makes some coffee for herself when her phone rings. Looking at the caller ID she sees it is Don.

"Hey, Don you back in town from Colorado?"

"Yes and I'd like to talk to you about a few things."

"Why don't you come over tonight, and we can have dinner together. How about seven o'clock?"

"Sounds good I'll see you at your place."

Putting the phone down she undresses, hops in the shower grabbing her coconut body wash, and wants to be ready for some fun tonight. When she is finished she dresses, rearms herself, and goes downstairs to bring back some food for dinner.

The appetizing food store is only a block or two down the avenue. The clerk remembers her from the last time she stopped in and asks if she would like some nova lox again. He received a new shipment in and can hand cut some for her if she likes.

"Yes I enjoyed it the last time. I need enough for two people, and a little for tomorrow's breakfast. I'll also take four everything bagels, some scallion cream cheese, and four cans of Dr. Browns Black Cherry soda please."

"How about our fresh baked chocolate Bobka also, you said you enjoyed it the last time you were here?"

"Yes, I forgot how much I enjoyed it. Okay, I'll take one too. I'll grab it myself from the counter over there, thanks."

Hurrying back to her apartment to slice the bagels, refrigerate the lox and cream cheese she starts to wonder what Don wants to talk to her about. Could it be regarding her being in Colorado while he is on assignment there too? Or does he need an answer at last as to whether she will move with him if he takes his promotion?

After putting everything away the concierge rings to announce she has a guest who wants to come upstairs.

Chapter Ten

Khara approves the unknown visitor without asking the concierge who is here to visit her and allows him to be sent upstairs. Don is expected and is supposed to be the one coming to be with her. Even though he is earlier than she wanted Khara doesn't mind. It has been a while since she has been with him in her bedroom.

When they met in the hotel at the registration desk in Colorado she couldn't chance to blow his cover, but now they can be alone.

The front door is opened, and she is surprised to find one of the CIA agents she met before she went to Colorado standing in the hallway, and not Don.

"Detective Bennet, can I come in I would like to speak to you for a minute?"

"Yes but make it quick I am expecting company soon."

"Thanks, I will try to make our talk as brief as I can. The FBI reported to Homeland Security you were in Central Oak Creek when the Chechnya leader Gretchen Pupovich hid out with some right-wing militias. The government of Bermuda needs to learn what you found out about her. Interpol is keeping her under surveillance as we speak. What can you tell us about the Chechen terrorist since you were with her before the militia's mountain base camp exploded, and went up in flames?"

"The woman the CIA is looking for is smart and cunning. In my opinion, if you ask me, she's too clever for you guys to catch up to her. The Chechnya rebels are dedicated and suicidal if cornered or caught. In the past few days, I saw too many Pupovich's die to believe she exists at all. The person in Bermuda is in all likelihood, not her. The terrorists want to bring the test tube with the virus back to Russia. The only real lead you might obtain, if she lives, is the woman who I shot in the O'Hare Airport terminal a day ago."

"My department posted security in her hospital room and hallway. The doctors said it is still touch and go if she will live. If she does we hope to gather more information from her. The vial is held out in front of you was filled with colored water. We don't know where the real stuff is hidden."

"Well, you'll need plenty of luck to motivate her to talk to you. I've seen women who claimed to be Popovich commit suicide right in front of me so they would not be coerced to speak to the authorities."

"There is no choice detective, you and your Russian landlord appear to be the only ones who actually saw her, and we want to fly both of you to Bermuda to try to meet with the Popovich Interpol is watching. The police are considering busting into her hotel room where she is staying, but they can't chance her opening the vial and letting the virus contaminate a whole island. The Governor of the island asked if you would be able to identify the woman, and maybe speak to her, and see what you can do."

"Sure, I need to clear it with my supervisor. No way will I turn down a trip to Bermuda if I can go for free."

"Not an issue we contacted her before I came here to talk to you. The Deputy Commissioner is fine with your going with us. Also, we have agents speaking to your partner as we speak. A private jet is waiting at Kennedy Airport to fly you both to Bermuda tonight."

"First I want to call my fiancé, and let him know what is going on."

"No need, we contacted him, and he is aware of the situation."

"Fine let me grab my backpack because I want to make a sandwich to take along. Only a few minutes ago I bought fresh bagels and lox. I'll eat it on the plane."

"There is no time to make a sandwich. Please take the food and put it in a bag. On the airplane you can make your sandwich, we need to go now."

Khara puts on her leather jacket, flips her arms through the backpack, takes her go-bag, and is ready to fly out tonight to Bermuda. Downstairs the agents parked a convoy of four black SUV's waiting for her and Olga. One of the other CIA agents contacted her, and she is in the lobby already. With their lights flashing and sirens blaring the convoy heads out to Kennedy Airport.

The task force pulls inside a private hanger by the airport's freight terminal, and sitting inside is a Bombardier Challenger 300 jet waiting for the agents, and both women to board. The CIA agents also walk up the steps to enter the plane. Everyone is seated as the jet taxis out of the hanger and takes its place on the runway for takeoff.

The flight is only a little over two hours. While in the air Khara pulls her tray table down, asks for a knife to cut the bagels, and puts the cream cheese and lox on two everything bagels. On a napkin, she places one, hands it to Olga, and also a can of soda after asking the CIA agent for a glass with ice. A button is pressed in and the seat goes back only slightly as Khara eats the bagel, and closes her eyes for a quick nap before arriving in Bermuda.

The landing is smooth, and when they disembark Khara asks the lead agent where they are staying.

"The agency booked rooms at a hotel in Saint David's Parish for you. Popovich is vacationing in a hotel in the area, and we are told she goes swimming every day near Clearwater Beach. This way you can be close enough to her to positively identify her to us."

"If she goes to the beach by herself why don't you arrest her? Why do you want me to identify her if you did it yourselves?"

"There are a few reasons we didn't move in yet. First, the Governor of Bermuda is afraid Popovich can disperse the virus and kill everyone on the island. Second we need to be sure she is who we think she is, and third, we believe there is an accomplice in the room with her. Someone is always in the room where we believe the vial is being held."

"How many test tubes does she possess? Do you know, or are you guessing?"

"In all honesty, we have no clue as to how many vials are in the hotel room. The Royal Government needs someone with your abilities to enter the room, and neutralize whoever is in the place with Popovich."

"It's now past midnight, and I need to inspect the grounds where she is staying, and what the topography of the area is like."

Soldiers of the Bermuda Regiment are present and escort both of them to Saint David's Parish where the hotel is situated. Although it is late at night the lampposts on the manicured lawns give off enough light where she can visualize the trees, hand trimmed brush and the gentle sloping of the property. In the silence of the night, she can faintly hear the water slapping against the rocks not too far away.

The washed out pink and pale green paint of the hotel is barely visible in the dark, and the color scheme is carried into the interior of the lobby.

The convoy stops at the front entrance, a bellhop hustles out to greet them with a baggage cart and take their bags to the registration area to sign in. The group walks past wicker and rattan furniture at the hotel and spa. A policewoman with the Bermuda Police Service is dressed in a hotel uniform and greets them from behind the massive hand-carved polished mahogany desk, and assigns each of them a room on the third floor. The room Khara is assigned to is next to Pupovich's so she can keep a better eye on her.

The elevator is only a few steps away from her room although Pupovich's is situated in front of it.

Once in the room her bags are placed on the dresser, she tips the bellhop, and she takes her coconut body wash out heading for a relaxing shower. This has been a busy day, and in the morning she can decide how to handle Pupovich.

***

The next morning she awakens about nine o'clock and calls Olga to find out if she is ready to go downstairs for breakfast.

"Sorry, I'm not dressed yet Khara. In thirty minutes or so we can meet in the lobby because I need to blow dry my hair. Okay?"

"Sounds good, I'm almost ready so you can find me in the lobby."

The weather is beautiful with the sun shining, and walking out on the veranda to her room she discovers the beaches below are not too far away. The early morning sun is beating down on her face, and the water is a calming blue color. Also, her balcony, situated next to Popovich's, is only separated by a few feet of air.

Back in her room, she puts on her ankle holster with her snub nose.38 in it, and in her right boot places the knife sheath. Both will be hidden by her thin slacks. The weather is too warm for her to wear the leather jacket. Now it is time to go down to the lobby and wait for Olga so they can eat breakfast together.

As Khara opens the door to her room to step out the elevator is on her left. The steel door slides open, the woman in the next room walks out at the same time and enters. From the back, she appears to be like the aid that was in the militia mountain base camp with Gretchen Popovich. The woman is dressed in a floral blouse and color coordinated plaid shorts.

With a quick two-step Khara is able to walk in the elevator before the door closes right behind her. The woman walks in first and her back is to Khara. When she turns to face the door there is an instant recognition between the two women. This person, Khara believes, fits the description perfectly as to what Popovich is supposed to look like. In her mind, this is definitely Popovich.

The shorter woman, without warning, pushes her arms straight out slamming Khara against the closed steel door. The push is followed up by an attack with a left kick. Turning to the side Khara grabs the woman's leg by the ankle as it goes by her striking the door. With a firm grasp she lifts the leg up and she flips the woman backward into the rear wall as the elevator starts to go down. Popovich jumps up, shakes off the cobwebs, assumes a combative stance and strikes out with karate punches while moving forward backing Khara closer to the elevator wall as she is deflecting the glancing blows to the side avoiding them hitting a vital spot.

Now assuming a defensive posture Khara is able to avoid the punches while waiting for her opportunity to strike back. In an instant her hand finds Gretchen's nose flattening it, and stunning the woman. Dazed Popovich is hit again this time with a roundhouse kick to the side of her face smashing her lips against front teeth causing deep red blood to flow down her chin, and a few teeth also fall out onto the floor. The force of the kick turned, and then slammed her head into the steel elevator door smearing fresh blood across the polished gleaming metal.

With her left hand, she reaches over, and Khara pulls the stop button out. The elevator jiggles a little and halts its descent almost at the ground level in the entry of the hotel.

The woman places her hand on the floor of the elevator trying to rise up when Khara kicks her arm out from under her causing Gretchen to again fall on the tile while breaking her wrist with the strike of her boot's heel. Popovich is kicked again, this time in the ribs. Khara drops her knee with all her body weight in the middle of Pupovich's back and grabs the hair on both sides of her head smashing it up and down multiple times splattering blood all over the elevator floor. Gretchen is dazed and moaning.

The punishment continues as Gretchen is grabbed by the hair on each side of her head, and again her face is pounded into the floor a few more times. The intent is not to kill Popovich but to disable her enough so no fight remains in her body. When Popovich is limp and motionless, spread-eagled out in the elevator and groaning the pounding stops.

With her right hand reaching down Khara takes her knife out of its sheath, and starts to cut off the pockets on Gretchen's shorts to inspect what she is carrying on her person. The left rear pocket contains a tissue and room key. With two hands she grabs her by the hair and twists her head around until she turns face up lying on her back.

The right front pocket is sliced open, in it, there is a mini wallet with some American dollars, and one credit card from Bank Rossiya, a Russian bank. The name on the card is Gretchen Popovich in English and Cyrillic. Khara cuts off the left front pocket but it is empty.

Her left-hand rips the woman's blouse open to complete the search, and try to find if any identifying tattoos are present. Not seeing any markings she inserts the blade under the white bra between her breasts and cuts upward. When the white cups fall to the side handwritten in black ink some numbers in one of them is found. Curious she slices off the inner cloth from the cup and places the piece of fabric in her pocket. Khara pushes the stop button in allowing the elevator to settle a few feet, and the door opens.

The police who are disguised as employees in the lobby run over to the elevator, and find a motionless woman lying in a pool of blood. The lead officer is aware who Khara is, and walks her out of the lift to a side room off the main entry. A screen is pulled over from the side entrance of the restaurant to block other guests from viewing the body in the elevator. An ambulance is called and a police detail escorts Popovich, handcuffed to a stretcher, to King Edward VII Memorial Hospital in Paget Parish.

***

In the small anteroom by the lobby, the police captain walks in and sits opposite Khara at a small table.

"Detective Bennet I am told by the CIA you are a capable officer, and teach self-defense to police recruits in New York City. Thank God you didn't kill her because we still need to find out why she is in Bermuda. The thought of her vacationing here we do not think is a valid one. Do you have any idea why she picked this island to stay?"

"Wish I could answer you. There are only two reasons why I think she would come here instead of going back to Chechnya. The first is she needed to hide out because Interpol is looking for her, and the Russian FSB posted a bounty out on her head either dead or alive. Also, I would double the security at the hospital, and do a background check on all personnel working on her floor. If they find out she is here they will attempt to kill her before you can question her."

"The second reason I can think of is the Chechnya rebels need money to finance their revolution. MI6 thinks vials could be in her room or hidden on the island somewhere so she can sell them. Try to keep the news of her arrest quiet until we know for sure. But if she is trying to sell the test tubes some unsavory guests will soon be checking into a hotel on Bermuda. How long is Popovich booked to stay here?"

"Our information is two weeks, and she is only here three days so far."

"Okay, you must try to find a female officer about her size who can take her place. Olga can speak on the phone for her since she is a native Russian speaker. The police need to wait and discover who registers, and from what country they come from. This island may become ground zero for terrorists to meet, and bid for the ultimate weapon of mass destruction."

"Unfortunately Detective Bennet I think you are correct. What are we going to do about the man who is staying in her room while she goes out. The room is never left unoccupied. What do you think?"

"The virus must be in the room somewhere otherwise they would leave the room together, and not individually. To be honest I understand why you don't rush the room. Whoever is in the room can open a vial and the whole island can be dead once the breeze blows in from the water. Give me a little while, and I'll have the room empty."

"What do you plan on doing?"

"I'm not sure yet, but I'll need to speak to Olga, and we'll work it out."

Shaking hands Khara turns, opens the door, and walks in the lobby to meet Olga.

"Good morning Khara I see you were busy before breakfast today. Let's go in and grab a bite to eat. I'm hungry, and it is still early in the morning."

The restaurant overlooks the manicured lawn with views out to the water in the near distance. Khara orders her usual coffee and buttered roll while Olga wants two eggs over easy with toast and tea. While they are eating Khara comes up with a plan to enter the room.

After paying and leaving a tip they both decide to walk up the stairs while the elevator is being cleaned due to blood splatter.

Once in their room Khara completely undresses, fluffs her short Afro-styled hair, and applies some makeup. Olga meanwhile unfastens the noise suppressor from the Velcro holding it to her holster.

The sliding screen door to the balcony is opened, and Khara takes in a deep breath of the salt air and walks out nude into the shining warmth of the sun. While she is doing this Olga screws the noise suppressor on her Glock and slides behind the floor to ceiling drapes by the door and watches. With a quick move to the right side of the railing, Khara stares into Gretchen's room and views a man looking out at the water. She waves hello to him and inhales again pushing out her chest, and he waves back. The man is taking the bait as he slides the screen door open, and steps out onto his balcony to talk to a beautiful naked woman who beckoned him with a hand gesture.

Standing at the furthest point on her veranda away from the building's wall the man must cross his balcony to come face to face with her. The distance between the balconies is only a yard or so. The man is smiling, and she thinks he is anticipating a good time. But the minute he stops and is facing Khara two bullets come flying out from Olga's pistol hitting him in the middle of his chest. The rebel is knocked backward off his feet and is lying on his back. Khara wastes no time and climbs up on the railing jumping across the small divide of air to Pupovich's balcony. Following her jump, Olga also makes the leap from her white ornate iron banister joining her on the terrorist's balcony.

Leaving his body flat on the floor they start to ransack the room searching for the vials. As an ex-KGB agent for many years, Olga was taught where to look.

Taking out the lowest drawers from the dresser she finds the Masonite bottom of the drawer is lying on the floor under the rattan dresser. On top of the Masonite, below where the drawer would slide are three test tubes. With utmost care, she starts to take them out motioning to Khara to bring a few towels from the bathroom to wrap each one by themselves. Working silently because they do not know if the room is bugged with listening devices they motion to go back to their room. Having secured two Olga leaves one behind where she found them with the bottom dresser drawer slightly pulled out so it would be noticed.

Olga jumps first, and Khara reaches across to hand her two towels with the sealed vials safely ensconced in thick cotton velour to prevent breakage if dropped. After this, she hops across to her side and walks in her room to dress before the police arrive.

Khara picks up the room phone and calls downstairs to the registration desk asking to speak to the police captain. Once he answers she identifies herself and tells him to come upstairs now to Pupovich's room. The authorities obtain a passkey from the management to every hotel guest room, and Khara walks out of her room to wait for the elevator.

"The white suits are not needed, guys. Relax I searched the room before you arrived, but you can open the door, and you'll see for yourself. There is nothing in here I could find."

"We'll check for ourselves Detective thank you."

A royal policeman opens the door, and they all walk in seeing the dead body spread out on the balcony. The captain glanced at the dead man and turns to Khara.

"You shot him, detective?"

"No, he tried to choke me when I hopped over onto his balcony. Olga saved my life and she shot him. You can see he is almost twice my size. The guy caught me by surprise because I thought he was in the bathroom."

With a fair amount of skepticism in his voice, the two are spoken to by the police captain.

"Luckily both of you carry diplomatic passports so you can't be charged. This incident will be buried in paperwork so it doesn't leak out to the press. In my command, I employ a female officer who is having her hair cut and dyed black. The policewoman is a natural blond and eyes are blue, no need for contact lenses. My Pupovich clone will be up here in two hours or sooner. How about I wait here with you two until she arrives? In case someone tries to reach Popovich by phone."

The other police officers start searching the room. The bed is torn apart, they go through their suitcases, some clothes hanging in the closet, and find nothing. One policeman sees the bottom drawer extended a little so he starts pulling it out, and spots the one test tube Olga left on the floor under the dresser for the police to find.

"I think I found a vial!"

Everyone backs away from the officer, and the men in hazmat suits approach it with gloves on and are about to place the test tube gingerly in an airtight sealed and secured riveted aluminum case. With care, they place the vial in a thick waffle foam lined suitcase and walk out of the room with it. The police parked a special bomb unit truck behind the hotel. With care, they place the small airtight trunk in the rear compartment, seal it closed, and drive off to their laboratory under serious security.

The hotel returns to normalcy with no apparent sign of a police presence.

Khara and Olga walk out to the balcony to speak privately after the man's body is removed by the emergency services unit.

"Hey, Olga I am aware you left one vial for the officers to find. What did you have in mind with the two we took back to our room?"

"When we go back home I am going to help you with the Mexican Colonel who is trying to kill me too. One vial you will bring back to Plum Island. The other one I am thinking of going to Mexico with, and take out the Colonel once and for all."

"Well, first we need to finish this assignment and find out who shows up for Gretchen's vials. In my pocket, I have a number I cut out of her bra in the elevator. It looks like a phone number to me but I haven't had time to research it. Last year I downloaded a software application on my cell where I can check phone numbers, but I want to walk away from the hotel.

The bidders might have a scanner which can intercept my transmissions. Let's go for a stroll it is pleasant out, and let the captain worry about someone contacting Gretchen. Listen we need two hours before his female officer shows up, c'mon let's go."

Taking the elevator down to the lobby they walk out the front entrance and turn left. There is a small walk through a thicket and eventually, it stops on a small mound overlooking a pink beach. The signage on the bottom of the path contains an arrow pointing to Turtle Beach. Khara can see the pink sand below and stops before they go on the beach. There is no one around so Olga takes out her mobile phone, and dials the numbers on the cloth into her keypad. The application comes back and informs her it is a conference call number, with a passcode after the hyphen.

"This is a conference call account. She must be auctioning the virus off to the highest bidder to help finance her revolution, you were right Khara."

"Big Boy needs to receive a text from me, and I must tell him to DHL something to me at the hotel overnight if possible. Because I need a solid uninterrupted internet connection it is important we walk back to the lobby now."

"Do you want to use my phone? Because I travel all over the world with Viktor I bought a satellite connection with my phone."

"Thanks but he needs to see it is from my phone or he won't answer the call and send me what I need."

The walk back goes quickly, and when she is on the veranda of the hotel she sends her text. Both of them sit on the beautiful rattan chairs and relax for a while until a message is returned from Big Boy. The message is he will buy what she needs, and send it out today.

"What did you ask him for Khara?"

"You won't believe what I wanted, but I told him to express me an antiviral gas mask."

"Honestly I think it makes sense."

"Could be, c'mon lets go to the bar and order us a cold beer. I'm thirsty."

They walk inside the lobby and turn to the left to an open doorway into the Old English style bar. Dark wood paneling is on the walls, a dartboard is hanging on a back wall, and the room is dark with the exception of the wood and glass open French doors leading to the veranda.

While seated at a small square table situated under a large ceiling fan the Chief Inspector of the Bermuda Police Service walks in, introduces himself to them, pulls out a chair, and sits to join them. They are in the corner of the room, and as usual Khara and Olga both are with their backs to the wall facing out to the veranda, and the bar entrance.

"Good morning ladies looks like you two had somewhat of an adventure in the hotel this morning."

Impressed a Chief Inspector would join them at their table Khara shakes his hand and welcomes him to the table. Olga is reserved and does not say much yet listens to what he is saying.

"First I want to welcome you to our peaceful island of Bermuda. Secondly, may I speak frankly to you both?"

"Please do Chief."

"Interpol's been in touch with the British MI6, and they sent me some background information on the two of you. I am glad you are on our side. But be careful. We learned you ladies are deadly and capable women whose fashionable appearance can be deceiving. Behind those smiles and high cheekbones are intelligent killers. MI6 told me you are here at the

CIA's request and have diplomatic passports, but I would rather work with you both than have to kill you while defending my island. What I am saying is work with me and not by yourself. If you go it alone signals can be mixed up, and through miscommunication, you could be in harm's way. The last thing I want to do is to send either of you back to the states in a body bag instead of a seat on a plane. Are we all on the same page?"

"Absolutely Chief, I am glad we had this little chat. I expect to receive from my sources a conference call phone number Popovich is supposed to use to set up a bidding auction for the virus. I should receive the number in a few days. Then Olga will make the call from Gretchen's hotel room. Your officers can be with us when we do. I am going to set a trap for the buyers, and I will need your assistance at the time of the winning bidder is meeting us."

"This sounds like we reached a meeting of the minds Detective. Here is my card with my private phone number, and make sure you call me when this is going down, understand?"

"Loud and clear, can I buy you a cold beer chief?"

"No thank you, but maybe when this is all over we can sit and enjoy a quiet dinner together, and talk about a few things?"

"Of course we can, and I look forward to it, thanks."

The chief stands and walks out of the bar to two plainclothes officers on his security detail waiting by the entrance for him to leave.

Finishing their drinks Khara suggests they call a taxi and take a tour of the island.

"Since we know no one is going to come calling for Gretchen until we make the conference phone call let's go out today and visit all the sights. When I came here on a cruise with Eloise we took a personalized tour with a taxi driver. In my contacts list, I have his number on my phone. Give me a second, and I'll contact him to pick us up."

Turning on the mobile phone she dials him, and he is available to drive them today.

"My tour guide will be here in thirty minutes Olga. Let's wait outside it's a nice day."

When he arrives he opens the rear doors and kisses each of them on the back of the hand and welcomes them to Bermuda. They climb in the back, and he takes them on a tour of the little-seen parts of the island tourists would not be shown.

The drive is leisurely and serene. Olga looks out in his side mirror and finds a car is following them at a distance.

"Khara I think we have a tail behind us."

"Not surprised. Dollars to donuts it is the police trying to keep tabs on us. They know we are here, and who we are. The chief as much told us in the bar. Relax and think of it as having our own security force protecting us from harm."

The taxi stops by a flowering bush with beautiful pink carnation-like flowers and the guide picks two from the bush explaining the genesis of the plant as he turns around in his seat, and hands one to each of them.

They each smell the flower, smile while sitting back, and enjoying the tour of the island. This is Olga's first time in Bermuda and the architectures and coloring of the homes she finds pleasant. The tile roofs which lead to a drainage system to collect rainwater she finds amazing.

"When this is over Khara I will take you to Cuba with Viktor and myself. There is a villa owned by the Cuban Secret Police on the island reserved for us. It's good to have friends in high places.

Chapter Eleven

Late the next day DHL delivers a medium size box to the hotel. Eager to access the package she does not wait and carries it up to her room. Her hand reaches down, removes the knife from her boot sheaf, and Khara cuts the flaps open lifting up the contents placing it on one of the queen size beds in the room.

Olga is wondering as to why Khara ordered this as she looks at her with a confused expression on her face.

"Can you please tell me why you asked him to buy this for you, and ship to Bermuda two gas masks? We are not opening any of the test tubes we are bringing back with us, are we?"

"No, not at the moment we're not. The truth is I might need this antiviral mask in the immediate future; you never can tell. I'm going to contact the Chief of Police we met yesterday, and ask him to bring his intelligence unit up here tonight. We are going to make the conference call to start things rolling."

The call to the police is made, and in a short time, Khara's room is filled with officers.

"Please, I need it quiet while Olga makes the phone call. She speaks with a Russian accent, and whoever is in on the conference call will not be set off by it; they will expect her to speak this way."

The handset to the phone is raised, and Olga dials the number from the fabric Khara places in her hand. The room is silent as she punches in the conference call numbers and waits for a connection.

One by one three voices sign on to the call using numbers which are, to Khara's way of thinking, assigned to them before the calls began for identification and security reasons. Olga presses the speakerphone button so everybody in the room can listen in.

"I want to thank you for bidding. You all are aware of the news reports on the Times Square New York terror attack. In two days I want payment delivered to me in Bermuda. This is where you can find me. I will be on Turtle Beach, near the airport, at nine in the morning on a blue blanket. The vials will be buried on the beach in an insulated bag a small distance away from me for security reasons. Remember when you deliver the diamonds to me I will point out where the test tube is hidden. Does everyone agree?"

One voice speaks up. "This is not the way you first instructed us. Why do we need to bring diamonds, and not pay by a wire transfer as you asked before?"

"Circumstances made the change necessary. If you want what I possess you will produce the cut diamonds in two days. Now let the bidding begin."

When Olga told the bidders the toxin will be on Turtle Beach in two days she laid a trap for the terrorists. The winning bidder will be there, but so will the losers in an attempt to steal the vial, and not pay for it. Olga told them nine o'clock in the morning because the area should be empty so no innocent civilians would be in their way.

The three bidders soon draw down to two. The winning bidder, to Olga's ears, talks with an accent she cannot place. Besides being fluent in Russian she speaks a few other languages. The winner, in a deep accented English, agrees to accept her demands. In two days the buyer will be in Bermuda to meet her as arranged. The last one is still on the phone. Before she hangs up Olga gives the winning terrorist a code word for when they meet on the beach, and the conference call is ended.

The police captain is in the room and asks Khara what her plan is to capture the bidding terrorists.

"First we want to buy a blue blanket for your Popovich clone to lie on, and another one in a different color for me. Plus we will need a large yacht anchored off the shoreline, and two wide sand umbrellas for the beach. A colorful one for her to sit under, a darker colored one for me and some Velcro to attach my snub nose .38 to the underside fabric."

Khara can see a puzzled look on the captain's face while she explains what her plan is.

"First your clone will go to the beach at dusk the night before and carry an insulated bag with her. She will bury the bag on the beach about thirty feet from the entry path. I am going to assume the three bidders will be having people watching the area like a hawk. With luck, they may try to snatch the buried bag before nine o'clock two days from now. By tomorrow they should be sending someone to Bermuda to be working as a lookout for them if they are not already on the island."

The captain is listening with care but still, there are some questions for her. "They are aware it is a beach so we cannot show any police on it, or they will spot us and flee. How do you plan to catch them?"

"As you know Turtle Beach is rather secluded behind a tree line. You will need police to be hiding at the restaurant on the bluff across the street. Also, I want squad cars hidden a block away. From the yacht you will arrange to be anchored offshore there will be undercover police on the boat in bathing suits with high-powered binoculars watching the shoreline. If someone comes on the beach with a shovel before your decoy arrives to let the police in hiding know. Once they dig up the insulated bag you call, it in and pounce on them before they can leave the beach."

"Also two days from now when your female officer will be on the beach I will be there too to protect her, about twenty feet or so away from her. My blanket will be located between your decoy and the entry path. My umbrella will hide my extra gun hung to it out of site. I will be sitting on a beach blanket, and near to me, my Sig Sauer will be under my bath towel with loaded clips in case I need them. On the boat will be Olga handling my sniper rifle with laser sights keeping both your decoy officer and myself safe."

The captain is able to overhear what she said and makes a comment to Olga.

"Well, at least it is a plan which makes sense. I'm not happy terrorists are on the island but we need to deal with reality. There is a resident I am friendly with on Bermuda who owns a mega yacht which should be stable enough if they drop anchor. How good a shot are you, Olga?"

"After I enlisted in the Russian Army I achieved the rating of a marksman, and the KGB sent me for sniper training lessons before I was sent out on missions. Remember this, I never miss my target."

The expression on the captain's face appears to Khara like he did not expect an answer like the one he received. He knows Olga is an ex-KGB assassin, and he would never expect to be face to face with one, ever.

"One more question Detective Bennet. Why did Olga ask for diamonds instead of cash?"

"First we don't know where the money via a wire transfer would be sent. Let's be real I don't think you would like terrorists to be able to send millions of dollars to their secret bank accounts stashed somewhere in the world. Plus diamonds are easier to carry rather than a ton of cash across borders. They can be here in two days with the jewels hidden in their pants pockets as they enter through customs."

"And what are you two ladies going to do here for the next two days while we set up our security details?"

"I think we will do a little shopping in Hamilton, some more sightseeing with our favorite tour guide, and a little relaxing around the pool drinking cold piña coladas, and twirling its small umbrella."

***

After lunch, Khara calls Johanna at her office at One Police Plaza to check in with her on what the situation is in Bermuda. She is explaining how a trap is being set to capture a group of terrorists. Johanna is satisfied and does not ask for her to return to the city.

Next, she calls her fiancé Don Weber at his FBI office in Manhattan to explain she is still away on assignment in Bermuda with the CIA and will be back soon. He is not thrilled with her being away.

"Look Khara I realize we are in law enforcement together, and sometimes we need to be on assignment somewhere else. The problem is when both of us are away at different times we don't see each other too often or enough. I'm not sure this engagement is going to work out for us, or if we decide to go ahead with the marriage. I want to settle down, and I don't see how our proposed marriage is going to be able to manage our kind of work and leisure lifestyle."

Being a clinically diagnosed psychopath Khara harbors no real feelings either way toward Don. Her psychiatrist Eloise did the diagnosis years ago.

"If this is how you feel about our engagement Don let's be adults, and call our marriage off. Listen, to be honest I understand the situation we are in at the moment."

"It is, I think, for the best. I will miss you Khara."

When she agreed with what he said to her Khara thought Don sounded a little dejected.

"I'll return the ring to you when I am back in New York."

"No, you keep it. I did harbor feelings for you, but I can't maintain a relationship like this. So I am going to accept the promotion, and move to the Midwest."

"Don I understand."

The call is ended as is her engagement. If he ever gets back to New York Khara will be glad see him for a night or two. The meeting will only be for carnal enjoyment, not for an emotional attachment or heartfelt memory. In a sensual sense, Don will be missed.

Khara, finishing her calls to New York, changes into a tiny bikini, and goes down to the pool to hang out in the sun. Before leaving her hotel room she goes into the bathroom and takes down a large bath towel. With care, she wraps her snub nose .38 in it, grabs her small pocketbook, and walks out to the elevator.

When she enters the pool area she spots an empty chaise under an umbrella, goes over and lays down to relax a bit. A waiter comes by, and she waves him over. Khara looks up at him through her sunglasses, and she orders a Piña Colada. The troubles of the planet are a world away from her at the moment.

In a few minutes, the young college age waiter with the six-pack abs brings over her cocktail, and she asks him to charge it to her room number. "Maybe tonight if you are not too busy you can bring me another drink after ten if you would like to join me?"

The young boy smiles, thanks her, and writes her room number down on his order pad.

A few minutes later Olga enters the pool area and lies on the chaise next to her.

"So how long did you stay in Cuba with Viktor? I never heard the story."

"The Kremlin assigned us to go to Cuba to assist Fidel. The rumor at the time is the garrison on the island of Cayo Piedra is going to assassinate him. A colonel stationed on the island to protect him is rumored to be fermenting unrest among his troops."

"So why didn't Castro send in some of his men, arrest the colonel, and end the problem?"

"He wanted to, but to arrest all the men he would need to bring more soldiers to the island. Only a select few people even knew the place existed. It is located about ten miles off the Cuban coast, and he ordered all maps not to show where it is. Castro felt the fewer people who know of the island hideaway the better for him. There is a mini mansion for him, his wife, and his five kids which face East out to the water."

"We flew to Cuba on a Russian airline. After we landed a Cuban Army convoy drove us to a small desolate fishing village near the Bay of Pigs where we boarded a skiff, and are taken out to sea to visit with Castro himself."

"You actually met him?"

"Yes he brought us to his house on the unknown hidden island, and we shared some expensive whiskey he served us himself. He gave Viktor a box of Uppman cigars to bring back with him. He knew we are there to take care of the garrison problem for him. We think Castro thought he is sending us on a suicide mission so he treated both of us like cherished guests. The difference is we knew what we are going to do. Our goal at the time is to take out the colonel first. Our handler in Moscow informed us the officer in question wanted to overthrow the regime, and declare himself president."

"Viktor asked for a driver to bring us out to the garrison so we could meet the colonel in question. The small camouflaged army jeep bumped along over dusty and rutted dirt roads to the other side of the island. The forest is dense and held the hot humid air close to the ground. By the time we arrived at the army compound, and it is only a twenty-minute ride, we are ready for a good long shower. When we finished parking in front of the cream-colored stucco building's entrance the driver waved to us and escorted us into the garrison office. There I saw a soldier is sitting behind an old wooden desk piled high with papers staring at the wall. When we entered through the doorway he too motioned us to continue through an old wooden door into an inner office. The colonel is an older man with a pencil thin mustache and a deep scar on the top of his forehead. He is sitting behind a stack of papers on his desk smoking a thick Cuban cigar with a fan circulating at a snail's pace above his head. I stood behind Viktor not moving. In a soft voice, I talked to him in my broken English and asked him point blank why he wanted to overthrow Castro. The colonel's face froze when I asked the question. The moment I spoke he recognized my Russian accent and must have realized why we are there to see him."

"I am peeking over Viktor's shoulder, and I saw sweat beading up on the colonel's brow. The colonel with no hesitation stood ramrod straight from his chair and glared at me. He sputtered to me what would be his dying words."

"I am a son of the revolution. He is a usurper and not one of the people. He lives like a king on this island while my wife and children struggle to feed themselves."

"At the point where he told us about his family not being able to eat, I saw him reach for a revolver on the desk. Viktor is standing in front of me, and the colonel could not see my gun is now drawn and hidden. I only needed one shot to finish him off. After I killed him I turned around, and when his security guards came running into his office I also shot all three of them in succession, no questions asked. Viktor grabbed a shotgun the colonel hung in his office behind his desk, a bandoleer of cartridges, and we climbed over the bodies in the doorway to leave.

"We strode out of the headquarters marching to the troop's quarters across a small open field. The sound of the shooting alerted the troops and a few soldiers came running out as we approached. I shouted in what little Spanish I speak to surrender. Most of the men stayed in their barracks, but the colonel's supporters came racing onto the barren compound to engage us."

"They are trying to shoot at us, but they never participated in actual combat, and looked afraid to me. Their aim is off because I found out later they did not practice an active shooting situation with blanks. Both Viktor and I many times in our travels experienced a real-life shooting position like this one in the past, and we are not nervous, but focused on our targets. As we continued to advance most of the troops stayed inside, or ran away into the woods, or are shot down if they came out of the building. The whole thing lasted maybe a half minute or so.

"The remaining soldiers walked out with their hands raised in the air. We ordered them to lie on the ground until more of Fidel's bodyguards arrived from the main house he lived in to take over for Viktor and me. When we are finished, and the rebel troops are secured our driver asked us to sit back in the jeep as we returned to Castro's mansion. As the vehicle turns away from the compound we listen to shots being fired one at a time behind us in what I would call a sequence."

"Back with Fidel for the evening, we are served dinner before we left on another boat. While we are dining with El Presidente he could not believe we took on a whole garrison of his soldiers and survived. Viktor thought it better not to tell him his troops are not trained as well since the Soviets stopped sending him support. The island suffered without their money and manpower. In gratitude, and maybe in fear of pissing us off, Castro gave us a villa on the main island to use whenever we visited Cuba. The Cuban secret police still maintain the place for us to this day."

After three hours by the pool, and three cocktails later Khara decides to go back to her room for an afternoon nap. It is rare for her to get a chance to rest so at the moment she is taking full advantage of her quiet time.

***

The morning, at last, arrives when the plan becomes a reality.

The evening before the arranged meeting a sixty-foot luxury yacht is anchored offshore by Turtle Bay. Below deck, the lights are kept off so from the beach you cannot see inside the cabin with binoculars. By one window is a policeman looking out, and acting as a sighter using an infrared scope to see if anyone is hiding in the woods behind the pink sand of the beach.

By the second opening is Olga standing with the sniper rifle, and laser sight on top. The size of the boat and the still waters will give her an advantage when focusing on a target.

The third window is staffed by a policewoman handling communications with the authorities on shore. Everyone on board is wearing an earpiece.

The police set up a wooden barricade by the small dirt entry path to the beach. Attached to it is a massive painted sign informing visitors the sand is closed. The Bureau of Tourism is replenishing the beach, and no one is allowed on it. The Chief did this to prevent any civilian casualties if things go wrong.

Finished about eight o'clock in the morning a small Bermuda Army truck stops on the road adjacent to the trees, and policemen in camouflage uniforms who are also in the reserve jump out. They walk into the woods and are instructed to lie still on the ground until orders are given to advance. Each one has issued an earpiece so they can coordinate with the operation. Their instructions are if shooting ensues they are to shoot to kill.

In the morning the Popovich police clone takes her time walking onto Turtle Beach carrying a small canvas insulated bag, a small hand trowel, blue blanket and a beach umbrella. She lays the blanket and umbrella on the pink sand and goes almost to the water's edge where she bends digs a small hole and places the small insulted bag deep in the sand. After digging she stands erect, goes back, sets up the colorful umbrella, tests the hidden microphone strapped to the metal folding arms, and spreads out a large blue beach blanket over the pink sand to sit on.

As soon as the Popovich clone is set Khara comes on the beach, and sets up her umbrella about twenty-five feet away from the policewoman. The blanket is placed between the clone and the entry path to the beach. The dark-colored umbrella is driven down deep in the sand and spread open shading her white blanket. On the underside attached to the fabric is her snub nose .38 held with Velcro, and out of plain sight. If she needs it the gun is accessible.

To psychologically make the men who might show up for the buy believe she is not a danger, and in their minds be at ease Khara is wearing only a tiny thong bottom, and takes off the top of her bikini. Stretching out on her white beach blanket her ebony body contrasts with it. At her side by her right hand is a small pile of towels with her Sig Sauer placed inside. In her left ear is an earpiece connected to a small device which appears to be a small radio.

Everybody is in place when the first bidders stroll past the barricade arriving early. The time is almost eight o'clock, and two men dressed in tan slacks and a plain white short sleeve shirt go on the beach carrying a small tote bag which appears full.

As they walk by Khara they look down and smile at her which she reciprocates.

They continue walking to the Popovich clone and speak to her in accented English explaining they are early. Olga believes she hears a German accent. When she lived in East Germany for a year on assignment for the KGB she learned the language. "Here are the diamonds where is the virus?"

All the people on the boat, in the woods, and in the hotel above the beach on a bluff is listening into the conversation. Along with the police chief as the policewoman attached a hidden microphone to the bottom of her umbrella Khara listens in also.

The decoy is a cool and collected individual, and glances up at them through her dark sunglasses, smiles but does not speak so they cannot hear her Bermuda accent. Placing her hand out towards them with her palm up she points with her other hand to place something in it. One of the men reaches in the bag and puts a diamond in her hand. Next to her towel is a jeweler's loop. She places it by her eye and holds the gem between her fingers inspecting it.

The nice thing about sand is you cannot detect the muffled sounds of someone running up behind you. With no forewarning, Khara is present and strikes one of the men on the back of his head with the butt of her pistol knocking him to his knees. When the second man turns to see what is going on she smashes him in his face with the barrel of her gun. The buyer is dazed as she kicks him in the groin causing him to also slump to the ground. With a roundhouse kick, she targets his head and knocks out a few teeth while his jaw shifts to the right. He is now flat on the sand moaning.

Facing the first man she hit she also kicks him in the nose with her heel shattering it, and causing him to fall backward, and not move.

The police hiding in the woods run out, grab the two men by their legs bringing them back to the thickest part of the trees, and in a secure manner bind them until later. They are handcuffed together around a tree for security purposes. Their bag of diamonds is secured to their ankles and taped shut with security tape. The troops hustled to take up their positions again. Khara walks back to her blanket and again places her Sig Sauer under the pile of towels.

At nine o'clock sharp three men now walk through a small path between thick overgrown bushes on each side of the entry leading to the beach. This is the only entrance to Turtle Beach other than swimming in from the water.

Three men go past Khara who is again stretched out almost naked, and she is sure they perceive there is no threat to them.

As they approach the Popovich clone one of them reaches into his pants pocket and takes out a single diamond. They are not carrying a bag of any kind.

With an American western accent, he tells her "the militia misses her, and would like to know why you ran away in Colorado."

With the presence of mind, she uses what she thinks is a Russian accent to answer the question. If they are European she could not do this. The policewoman did not go to Colorado with the militia and does not understand what they are talking about so she tries to fake it by changing the topic.

"Where are the rest of the diamonds? Do you think I am stupid?"

The man closest to the water pulls a gun out of his pants pocket and points it at her forehead.

A shot rings out, and a bullet smashes through the left side of his head, and out the other side also hit the man standing next to him. Olga did understand what he said, and the sighter who is on the boat next to her instructed Olga to aim at the man with the gun so he can be taken out.

The remaining man reaches into the waistband of his slacks and starts to pull out a gun. This terrorist is shot in the back by Khara sitting only twenty-five feet away as she is running to aid the policewoman.

From the woods, the soldiers again come rushing out and drag away the three bodies. Later the men can be sent to either the hospital or morgue, but at the moment the police chief does not order them removed. Two of the policemen kick sand over the blood and brain matter on the beach to hide it.

The policewoman speaks up into the bottom of the umbrella where the microphone is hidden and asks if they are finished for the day. Khara responds to her to stay a little while longer.

"There were three bidders at the auction, and only two so far are able to show up. Plus none of the two mentioned the coded phrase. These guys are the losing guys trying to steal the vial. I think we should wait a while. It is still early in the morning."

Khara goes back to her blanket and lies down on it again tanning herself.

Nine-thirty passed, and the time is approaching ten in the morning when a group of seven men walks through the brush on the narrow path to the beach. Khara glances up at them, and half of the men are wearing long beards while the others are cleanly shaven except for one with a mustache.

They all are wearing dark slacks, not jeans, and patterned shirts, not tucked in their pants, which went out of style ten years ago. To anyone who lives in the modern world they stuck out as foreigners from a third world country. Some wore leather sandals but most are wearing shoes, not sneakers.

As they passed Khara they all stared at her but kept walking except for one clean-shaven younger man who appears to be in his mid-twenties. He is the only one in the group who smiled at her as they marched by the white blanket.

Turning her head to follow them she saw a slight bulge on their hips from under their shirts. They are armed. Khara slides her hand over to the pile of towels and grips the pistol in her fingers. The sun is beating down on her but she focuses on the seven men...waiting for them to make a move.

The younger man who smiled at Khara is carrying a small canvas bag which is bulging out from the sides. The bag must contain the diamonds she thought to herself.

The leader of the group approached the Popovich clone and stopped a foot or two away from her colorful umbrella. With a heavy accent, he told her their van is sabotaged, and would not start this morning. During the night somebody stole the distributor cap, and they needed to call two taxis to bring them all here together. "This is the reason we are late."

All the police hear him say this as he is only standing two feet away from the hidden microphone under the umbrella fabric.

Again trying to use her fake Russian accent she said only one word.

"Password?"

The leader of this group responded with the passcode words Olga told him after the auction is over. "Dead girls don't die."

Placing her left palm out to them she picks up the jewelers loop with her other hand.

Without speaking they know what she wants to do. The younger man opens the bag and takes out one diamond. He drops it in her hand being careful not to touch her. Putting a diamond between her fingers again she puts the jeweler's loop by her left eye and appears to look at it with care.

"Look at it all you want. The Ayatollah sent this package here for you. He would not cheat you or lie. He admires what you did to the infidels in America."

"Okay, it's buried down by the water. If you all line up and walk to the water's edge one of you should be able to feel it below your feet."

The younger man with the diamonds stays behind to guard her and the diamonds while the others head for the water as instructed.

Once there is some distance between the policewoman and the six terrorists the troops come running out from the woods yelling for them to raise their hands. The men turn, pick up their shirts from the bottom, and pull out their weapons.

The leader is shot dead by Olga from the boat and the bullet penetrates his body and burrows into the pink sand. The younger man takes out his gun and starts to run for the path leading off the beach, and toward Khara.

Seeing him running to her waving a gun she raises her Sig Sauer, and with two shots blows him away. His feet fly up into the air as he falls backward still clinging to the canvas bag. Khara reaches up and grabs her snub nose, and with two guns spitting out bullets of death she calmly walks to the waterline where the terrorists are focused firing at the troops.

In a matter of seconds, everything is quiet again.

Walking back to her blanket Khara pries the young man's clenched fingers off the canvas bag, picks it up, and places it on her blanket under her towels and out of sight.

A police captain emerges from the woods and calls for the Chief of Police to come down to the beach. In a matter of a minute or two, he is walking the narrow path and is standing by his policewoman. Khara puts the tiny bikini top back on and is about to fold her umbrella when the police captain walks over to speak to her. The chief is within earshot but stays a few feet away listening.

"Detective Bennet you and Olga did a good job here today. We caught three terrorist organizations."

"You do know captain there is no honor amongst thieves or terrorists. Two of the groups tried to steal the test tube from the winning bidder."

"Yes, I am aware of it. Besides, we took one bag of diamonds from them, where is the other one?"

"The other one is going back to New York to help the victims of the virus attack on Times Square."

"Sorry I can't allow you to take them back, Detective."

"Captain, I want your word you will not interfere with us bringing the jewels back with us. By the way, there is a spot on your shirt."

Looking down he can view a red dot from a laser bouncing up and down on his chest from Olga's sniper rifle.

"I think you know what it is Captain. I want your word you will let us go back to help innocent people heal. You control one bag which should be more than sufficient."

The chief of police overheard everything and turns to Khara.

"Ignore him, Detective. I will escort you to the airport myself. Let's all go back to the hotel so you two can pack. There will be a police convoy taking you to the plane."

***

Seated in first class thanks to the Bermuda Government's persuasion Khara and Olga are on their way to New York. Khara placed the bag of diamonds on the floor between her legs, and Olga is holding the two vials with the virus on her lap in her pocketbook. After the plane is in the air Khara asks her two questions.

"Why did you use the coded words the CIA told me?"

"To be honest I needed something on the fly, and those nonsense words came to mind."

"Tell me I am curious how much is the winning bid for the vial?"

"I settled for eighty-five million dollars."

"Now I know why only a rogue nation could pay so much for it."

The rest of the flight is in silence, and the plane lands without incident. Viktor is at the airport to greet them with his security team, and a limousine to bring them home.

Back in Brooklyn, all three are going up together in the elevator when Viktor asked if they could take their rent in diamonds.

Khara opens the bag; he reaches in and removes a handful of gems.

"Okay, now you can live here rent free forever."

When the elevator stops on her floor Khara walks out and goes into her apartment. Checking the security light she walks to the kitchen counter, opens a drawer, and withdraws a small handful of diamonds for her efforts.

Chapter Twelve

"Johanna I need you to send a hazmat unit to my apartment and pick up a vial of the virus I brought back from Bermuda. Also, I suggest in the strongest terms you come with plenty of armed security as I acquired a bag with almost fifty million dollars in diamond. The gems can be used for the Times Square victims because I confiscated them from the terrorists."

Focused on the deadly virus Johanna initially ignores the gems.

"So you brought the test tube back with you? Isn't it dangerous? What if it opened on the ride back to New York?"

"There is nothing to worry about if the test tube did open during the flight. The plane would crash land in the Atlantic Ocean, and there would be no problem with the vial ever again. But it didn't, and I am sitting with the last one in my apartment."

Khara understands another vial is safe and secure in Olga's penthouse apartment. In her mind, she plans to use it in the future, but at the moment nobody else is aware it exists.

"I will be at your place soon Khara. In ten minutes I am leaving my office, and I ordered the Brooklyn district commander to enable sufficient uniformed personnel to meet me at your apartment house."

Almost immediately squad cars begin arriving on the street in front of her home. A blockade is instituted with no traffic allowed to pass, including pedestrians. Shortly after a hazmat truck drives up, and a trailer full of wooden barricades trails behind it. Police institute a lockdown on the avenue and people who live in the area are instructed to stay indoors until further notice. The news media is informed a potential gas leak is present so nobody would panic. To reinforce the image a little stronger a Brooklyn Union Gas truck was brought to the corner and parked next to the barricades.

Ensconced in her apartment Khara starts to clean her weapons waiting for Johanna to come in. About thirty minutes after the phone call the concierge in the lobby calls upstairs to announce the Assistant Commissioner on Terrorism is here to see her. With a push of the intercom button, she tells him to please allow her to come up to her apartment.

The doorbell rings and Johanna is welcomed inside along with an armed twelve officer swat team. They walk into the living room and spread out holding their weapons waiting for instructions.

Now placing her unloaded guns on the kitchen table she walks into her bedroom with Johanna to retrieve the bag with diamonds. Once they are secluded inside her walk-in closet, away from prying eyes where the jewels are hidden, Johanna turns and kisses Khara.

"I'm so glad you're back safe, I missed you."

"And I missed you too. Why don't you stay after everyone leaves?"

"Today I can't, sorry. The commissioner needs a full report from me when I get back to headquarters, and I am expecting to hear from MI6 regarding your Bermuda adventure. How about I come back after work, and we can go out for dinner in Brooklyn?"

"Excellent idea, call me before you leave the city so I can get dressed."

Leaning around Johanna, and reaching behind some blouses Khara grabs a canvas bag full of diamonds to place it in her hands. With the gems secured, and in police custody both walk back to the living room.

The lieutenant in charge of the swat team is given the bag, and a secure lock is placed on the bag's handles. The officers leave the apartment and are going back to One Police Plaza in Manhattan with Johanna.

Once the swat team leaves the hazmat group enters, and the lead officer for the unit is handed the vial. A foam-lined aluminum case is opened, and the test tube is placed in the middle as the cover is closed, and is airtight. The latches are secured when they too leave the apartment, and they mention to Khara they are driving to Plum Island to bring the virus back to the lab where it belongs.

Alone in the apartment again she calls Junior to arrange a face to face meeting. Next on her agenda is the Mexican Secret Police Colonel. They agree to meet at the diner near Sheepshead Bay for lunch.

"Is Big Boy bringing you to the meeting today?"

"Yes, he is, why?"

"Because I want him present. He will, I assume, be needed for Mexico."

Back at the kitchen table Khara hangs up the phone and sits while continuing to oil her weapons. The throwing knife is cleaned, and hand sharpened almost to a razor's edge. After she is finished everything is put away and makes a fresh cup of coffee. The television is flicked on, and she starts to watch a national news channel.

It is almost time to go when Khara calls downstairs to the concierge and asks for her M3 to be brought to the valet stand.

After putting her firearm in her shoulder holster, her arms through a trusted leather jacket with the snub nose .38 in the right pocket she locks her door sets the alarm and heads down to the lobby.

The repaired M3's engine is rumbling waiting for her at curbside to throw it into gear, which she does with joy once she sits behind the wheel. The clutch is released as the gas pedal is smashed down forcing the black car to lurch forward with the engine pulsating under the control of its master behind the wheel. The radio is blasting a favorite Rolling Stones mix from her mobile phone as it moves along the streets heading to Sheepshead Bay.

With a quick turn into the parking lot she pulls into a spot in the last row way in the back, and next to Junior's red Cadillac. This is the one he inherited from his father and is parked by the back wall also. Khara exits her vehicle and makes sure her Sig Sauer is loose enough in her shoulder holster in case she needs it in an instant.

Walking up the six front steps to the diner she enters, spots Junior and Big Boy drinking a beer in a secluded corner booth, and starts to walk toward them. The maître d keeps the adjacent tables empty as usual due to a generous tip when they walked in the dinner.

While Khara approaches the table Junior is waving to her and is smiling. Big Boy is sitting facing out to the street and is not aware she is near until Junior stands to welcome her.

"Glad to see you again Khara how is Bermuda? Come sit over here where you can face the door, I remember your seating preferences."

"Thanks, Junior, hey Biggie how're you doing?"

"Fine Khara, I'm keeping busy with stuff, and you?"

"I'm okay. Let's order first because I want to let you guys in on what I have in mind."

In one easy motion as she sits on the booth's seat her body bends while scanning the underside of the table looking for hidden microphones.

The waitress comes to their table, and Khara orders a cheeseburger deluxe, medium well. Junior asks for egg omelet, and Big Boy orders an open turkey sandwich with mashed and mixed vegetables. The girl leaves to enter the food in the computer system and let them do their business in private.

"To finish off the Colonel I plan on going to Mexico City. With a diplomatic passport, I can carry what I need with me, and not be searched or stopped. Your part in this is to lease a villa near their headquarters for me, and for Big Boy to keep it secure. Money talks south of the border and life is not valued. I don't want one of the secret police hit men to wait inside for me as I walk in the villa, and be whacked."

"Easy enough to lease the home Khara but I can't send Big Boy with you. For my protection, I need him here, and for enforcement issues. Tiny is still in training with him and not ready yet to go out alone. With my father gone some of our clients are getting selfish with their money. Is there someone else you can bring with you? Maybe Olga might be able to go with you?"

"Not a problem, I'll speak to her. Can you reactivate the American Express credit card your father gave me to help cover my expenses?"

"Consider it done. My secretary at the funeral home will call them this afternoon to make sure it is still valid. Anything else I can do for you Khara?"

"Yes, pay for lunch, thank you."

With a smile, Junior laughs and sits back as the waitress brings their food order to the table. The diner is packed with people, and every booth is taken except for the two adjacent to the one where they are sitting. With a wave of his hand, pointing to those empty tables Junior tells the maître d she can now sit people at them. His business is finished. Within a few seconds, all seats in the place are full of hungry patrons.

The diner is situated in a middle-class Brooklyn neighborhood populated with a decent demographic of the city's ethnic populations. So when two cars stop in front, and five men hop out to walk into the lobby nobody notices anything out of place. All the young men appear as if they fit into the mix.

Once in the inner lobby, they take out their guns, and one of the young men rushes behind the counter to empty the cash register. The other four split up into teams of two, and each team takes a side of the diner. The robbers are going from table to table as they demand wallets, jewelry, watches, and rings from the people sitting in the booths.

The hostess is told to lie down on the floor. The gunman points his pistol at the cashier, tells her to empty the register, and yells at her if the silent alarm is set off she will die first if a cop shows up. The woman starts to cry not able to control her emotions.

Diners who are too slow are pistol whipped across their head, and their valuables ripped off their bodies. People are screaming and hysterical with tears running down their cheeks as the robbers run from table to table collecting money, watches and anything they think is of value.

With her back to the wall, Khara views everything going on in the place. Placing her hand in the right jacket pocket she takes out her snub nose, and under the table places it in her left hand. With her other one she reaches in, and grabs her Sig Sauer sliding the barrel back to cock the hammer; she is ready.

Two of the young robbers approach the corner table to rob them, and Khara slides out of the booth standing in the aisle facing them armed, her legs spread in a ready to shoot stance. Without a word being said her guns are ablaze with accurate aim as bullets spit out finding their mark. The two men in her section of the diner fall to the floor with multiple wounds to their body. Big Boy is now out of the booth and walking beside Khara as they head for the entrance doors to head off the other team in the place.

The holdup man stuffing the cash from the register in a bag glimpses them approaching out of the corner of his eye, and raises his gun. His first shot hits Big Boy in his chest flipping him backward on top of a roundtable where four elderly women are seated causing everything on it to tip and fall over. The food and drinks shatter on the floor with Big Boy landing on top of the mess face down. The robber behind the cash register never is given a second chance to fire. Facing the shooter one bullet from Khara's Sig Sauer hits him in the forehead, and he falls backward into the dessert display causing the pies and cakes to tip over to the floor, and land on top of his sprawled out body. The bag of cash and his pistol are lying next to him behind the counter.

The loud sounds of the gunshots echo off the glass windows and tile floor further upsetting the diners at their tables.

The other two robbers hear the shooting and run out of the serving area into the rear kitchen after seeing

Khara with her gold shield hanging around her neck blocking the front entrance so they cannot leave. Through the glass circle in the swinging kitchen entry and exit doors, she spots the robbers and chases after them. The cooks and dishwashers duck as the two men turn to shoot her as she runs through the double doors. Their bullets ricochet off the forest of chrome and stainless steel shelving poles preventing them to obtain a clear shot at her.

The two gunmen spot the kitchen exit, run through it, and into the parking lot where they split up going in different directions. Now realizing each robber is going a separate way she sprints after them. One of them is holding a bag, and she decides to go after the one with the stolen property.

The gunman runs into the street as one of their getaway cars squeals around the corner and stops in front of the gunman to allow him to open the door and hop in. The chase halts as Khara raises her Sig Sauer aiming at the passenger side of the car, and with care takes aim. One, two, three hollow point bullets spit out of the barrel of the Sig Sauer, and the robber is hit as he enters the car. The first shot hit him in the middle of his back smashing into his spine causing him to fall to the black asphalt in a fetal position grimacing in pain before he could sit in the front seat. The second shot misses bounces off the car's center console transmission shift rod damaging it and forcing the car's transmission to slide into park. The third bullet hits the driver in his right hand on the steering wheel tearing through it from the side of his hand by the pinky breaking bones in his hand and knuckles. Blood is pouring out as he holds his hand to his chest moaning in agony.

In a mad dash approaching the getaway vehicle, she can hear another car make a quick turn onto the avenue, and the remaining robber across the street hops in the rear door as the car speeds away.

Sirens can be heard blaring as they approach the diner. Police and ambulances race to the scene while Khara handcuffs the driver of the car to the steering wheel securing him until reinforcements arrive. Before leaving she also takes the ignition fob lying on the console. She steps over the other robber ignoring him lying in the street backing out of the vehicle. With her gold detectives badge out of her blouse she holsters her gun and places the snub nose back inside her jacket pocket. A quick bend down, and she grabs the bag of loot to keep it safe as she turns and runs to her M3.Without thinking she takes off from the other side of the parking lot after them.

On the hands-free phone in the car she voice dials Johanna to tell her what went down in the diner, and what she is doing at the moment.

"I'll call the district command and report in what you said Khara. Tell me where they are going, and I'll try to order a roadblock be set up somewhere."

"Now they are on the Belt Parkway heading east to Kennedy Airport. In two minutes we will be by Mill Basin, and the bridge to Far Rockaway."

"Okay I need you to keep this call open, and I'll inform the district where they are headed."

The getaway car is weaving in and out of traffic as the robbers are cutting off cars driving at high speed. The M3 is following as best it can without switching on a siren or flashing lights. At the moment Khara is aware the shooters don't realize she is behind them in her black BMW. She hopes they may slow down, not thinking about them causing any harm to anyone else, but so she can overtake them.

Flatbush Avenue is coming up fast, and the robbers veer off the highway heading for the bridge.

With a flip of a finger her turn signal goes on, and the M3 downshifts to third while swerving to the right to exit onto the street.

The getaway car begins to slow down as the toll booths come closer. They speed up and shatter the barrier speeding onto the peninsular sending splinters of wood flying into the air and doing damage to their hood and radiator grill.

The M3 slows down as she glides through the toll booth and starts to pick up speed to follow them into Reis Park. The last time she drove in the park with an M3 the drug cartel tried to kill her and shot up her old BMW. Today might be different. There is no way they will be shooting at her car if she can help it.

Driving on the perimeter road around the immense parking lot she observes them stop by a parked car on the far side of the last lot. They must have planned to change vehicles and left this one in the commuter lot before the robbery. Sure enough, they run out of their vehicle and jump in the parked one, and attempt to drive off.

Johanna is still on the open line while she explains what is going down. The local precinct and highway patrol vehicles converge on the parking lot and block all exits. The M3 pulls next to the squad cars as Khara stops and jumps out with her gold badge still hanging around her neck and a pistol in her hand.

The robbers start their car and speed toward a curb trying to jump the eight-inch height of a walkway concrete island to make their escape. The front of their car hits the solid sidewalk with such force the tires explode out, deflate, and the chassis is stuck on the island incapable of moving. With the police surrounding them, the two robbers opened their rear trunk, walk to the back of the car, and reach in with each man in a slow and calm manner taking out an assault rifle. Armed to the teeth they split off walking toward a different squad car firing as they approach.

Huddled behind their squad cars for protection, and outgunned the officers try to fire back. The police are shot at with automatic fire every time they raise their heads to see where to shoot. A quick dive to the ground and lying on the pavement Khara peers under the chassis of her car, and spots one of the robbers coming toward the M3 while he is shooting at the squad cars. The pocketbook is swung around and she reaches in and takes out the hand grenade which is always with her and pulls the pin.

When he is within her throwing range she heaves it over the car. There is an explosion, and shrapnel flies in all directions piercing through the metal on all the police cars and the BMW.

The automatic gunfire stops from this assailant. His partner is fast approaching the other side of the parking lot where the rest of the squad cars are blocking the exit. Khara and the officers near her stand and begin shooting at the back of the other robber. A fuselage of shots rings out; he is hit in the back of his head and legs and falls short of reaching his goal.

***

After the tow trucks load all the shot up police cars including the M3, and the ambulances leave, an unmarked car from headquarters drives onto the parking lot bringing Johanna to Reis Park. She is waving to Khara to come in the back seat so the police can drive both women back to Brooklyn.

On the ride back she brings Johanna up to date on the day's happenings. The reason she is in the diner is omitted on purpose, but the rest of the events are reported in a truthful manner for the most part.

The valet opens the rear door allowing both of them to exit the car, and walk to the entrance of Khara's apartment building. Johanna's security team is sent for dinner until called back in the morning. Once in the elevator Johanna turns to her, pulls her close, and whispers in her ear "glad you were not harmed."

With a halfhearted smile, Khara kisses her and takes out her keys from her pocket as the elevator reaches the fourth floor. Once inside they decide to order pizza for dinner and stay in the apartment for the evening. In her front pocket, she can feel a buzz on her phone so she opens it and reads a text message from Junior to please call him as soon as possible.

"Excuse me Johanna, but I need to take this call."

Walking to the living room window Khara presses her speed dial, and Junior answers.

"Hey Junior, its Khara, how's Biggie?"

"Big Boy is dead. The bullet from the robber pierced his heart. Go to Mexico, I'll pay for everything, and I activated your credit card again."

"Thanks, consider it done. I'll contact you when I get back."

Putting the phone in her front pants pocket she turns to walk back to Johanna.

"Is everything okay Khara? After the phone call, you appear to me a bit shook up."

"Yes, I am surprised, nothing else. One of the men in the diner who was shot today died. I knew him, and didn't expect the guy to go out this way."

There is no sadness in her voice, no emotion, only a matter of fact coolness. Big Boy is the last contact she kept from her days dating her old crime boss boyfriend Al, except for his son Junior.

The concierge is ringing, and Khara calls downstairs.

"Our pizza is here Johanna. He'll be up with it in a minute."

Johanna takes out money for the food, and when the doorbell rings she opens the apartment door to pay for the pizza. Standing in front of her is a young Chinese man delivering the hot pie. After tipping him she brings it to the table and calls out to her. "C'mon let's eat while the pie is warm."

The two sit at the kitchen table after Khara takes out some cold beer from the fridge and places dinner plates by their respective chairs.

"An amusing thing Khara is I find a Chinese guy delivering Italian food in a Russian and Jewish neighborhood. Don't you?"

"Nope, I never noticed. So tell me what information did MI6 send back to the commissioner on my Bermuda trip?"

"An interesting report was sent to me this morning. The Mayor called me into a meeting with him and the commissioner after I received the results from the British. It may be the woman you almost killed in the elevator might be Gretchen Popovich, but they are not sure. The person in the hospital matches her description in every physical way possible, but her fingerprints have been distorted so they cannot be traced back. Bermuda police detained her under tight security, and the Russians want her extradited to Moscow. The doctors are not sure she will survive the beating you gave her let alone be well enough to travel."

"You do remember she did try to kill me in the elevator. The unfortunate thing for her is she did not succeed."

With her left hand Johanna reaches across the table, and with gentle strokes brushes the side of Khara's face. The caring emotions from her behind this loving gesture is lost on Khara.

"Is there some way the city can repay you for what you did for us? I do know a commendation is in the works and will be given to you by the Governor and Mayor."

Without hesitating, Khara answers her question.

"First thing is if you can repair my M3 the police towed away today? Second I want a week or so vacation, I would like to go to Mexico to relax on the sunny beaches. Do you think you can swing those two items for me?"

"Consider them done. Tell me when do you want to travel to Mexico?"

"If I can I would like to go tomorrow, but I must speak to my landlord first, and see if she can go along with me."

"Would you rather I go with you Khara? We can enjoy a relaxing time down in Mexico together."

"To be honest with you I would love for you to go with me, but not now. This time off you don't want to ask me about."

"Yes I understand, you don't need to paint a picture for me. The next trip both of us can go, and spend some quality time together?"

"There is no doubt in my mind we will go on vacation. Let's go shower we both must get up early tomorrow."

***

The next day at six in the morning an unmarked police car stops at the yellow valet line and picks Johanna up in front of the building as she leaves for work. Once she is in the vehicle, and the apartment is empty Khara calls upstairs to the penthouse to speak to Olga, and asks if she can travel to Mexico with her to finish off the colonel once and for all?

"When do you want to leave Khara this is not a problem?"

"I'll try to book a flight to Mexico City for some time later today."

"One quick question first, do you have a plan?"

"Before I did, but Big Boy was killed yesterday. Now I guess I'll need to go into his headquarters and kill him myself."

"Not much of a plan you know."

"Sometimes the simplest thing works best. The Colonel doesn't know we are coming, and I remember where they hide out most of the time. I was to their safe house in Nuevo Laredo before, and we can take them by surprise."

The call is ended, and they both start to pack.

Khara always tries to carry extra ammunition with her and makes sure her guns are loaded. In the backpack is her MP7 machine gun with a few full clips. Placed in the small suitcase between her clothes, in parts are the sniper rifle, scope and a handful of bullets. She again fills the small pocketbook with one hand grenade and a few loose .38 cartridges for her snub nose.

Aero Supremo Mexico lists a direct flight out of Kennedy to Monterrey, only a short distance to Nuevo Laredo on the American border. Two first-class seats are booked online, and the pair is ready to leave.

Viktor instructs his limousine to wait out front to bring them to the airport. The two women are about to enter the vehicle when he tells them about a contact he is friends with in the United Nations Cuban Consulate in New York. His source will arrange for a guide and car for them when they land in Mexico.

Understanding this Khara realizes the individual picking her up needs to be more than a tour guide. The person waiting for them will be hired by a Cuban agent whose job will be to safeguard Olga. This is alright with her, since she will be with both Olga and the guide, and appears to feel like an extra gun is also coming along.

The limousine pulls out and is on the Belt Parkway heading east to Kennedy Airport. The vehicle arrives at the departing level in record time. The driver double parks pops opens the trunk and places their luggage on the sidewalk for them. With her weapons of death in the bags, she does not want them out of her sight as she waves the porters away.

The airline's office is on the second level. Both go into show their diplomatic passports and tickets. None of their luggage is searched, and they are allowed to enter the terminal.

Their flight is not leaving for an hour so they buy some bottles of water to carry on with them, a light sandwich, and two small bags of potato chips. Walking to the gate they see a few empty seats by a window and settle in until it is time to board the plane.

"If you remember the last time I flew on a Mexican airline the Ecru Cartel knew I was on the airplane, and the bastards tried to kill me. So I would not be surprised if the Secret Police placed me on a watch list, and are aware we are coming to get them."

"Yes, you could be on to something Khara. Years ago when I worked for the Kremlin the KGB used to do the same thing. If someone we wanted flew on an airplane from one of the airlines we controlled, anywhere in the world, we would be waiting for them when they arrived."

"I'm thinking the same thing. We are on a five-hour flight so might as well relax until the plane lands. Nothing we can do at the moment. Before we land make sure your gun is easy to withdraw from its holster."

It is a smooth flight with no turbulence, or assassins on the plane trying to kill them. The jet arrives safely and they disembark into the bowels of the terminal. A woman is waiting for them holding a sign with their names on a small chalkboard. The Mexican guide introduces herself, says she is here at the request of the Cuban Embassy in Mexico City and tells them in Spanish rooms are reserved for them in a small local safe house.

Speaking fluent Spanish Khara thanks the woman, and they grab their bags to follow her out to the waiting vehicle. The thought ran through her mind the guide appears surprised when she spoke error-free Spanish to her, but she doesn't say anything else.

It is a late model Japanese van they walk over to, and they pile in with their luggage. The guide enters the vehicle, sits behind the steering wheel, and pulls out heading for the Route 85 highway.

A short distance out of the city they stop in Ciénega de Flores where a safe house is reserved by the Cuban Consulate in Mexico for them to sleep in for the night. Before leaving Brooklyn Viktor made a few calls to arrange this for them.

The guide explains it is too dangerous to travel the highway after dark. Nuevo Laredo is only a two-hour drive, and in the morning they will leave at daybreak. There are too many banditos between the two cities, and you cannot spot them in the dark of night.

Khara is never bothered by a gunfight. One of her failings is she is an adrenaline junkie, and excitement is a thrill to her, not a danger. But Olga would rather be in a controlled situation if possible so the three stay in the safe house for the night.

There is a high wall surrounding the home with motion detectors discretely set on the roof aiming in all directions. The elderly woman who lives there walks with a limp and is the caretaker and cook. Her guests are shown to their rooms, and told a hot meal will be ready in a short time. After placing her bags in the bedroom Khara steps out to the living room and sits to stare at a motion detector security camera screen set high on the wall. There is a small television in the house along with an internet connection to the outside world.

In a minute the Mexican guide enters with her laptop and sits on a chair opposite Khara.

"Detective Bennet I read all about you last week from our files. You are a courageous person. We know last year you took out the Ecru Cartel by yourself. If you don't mind I do want to ask one question of you."

"Go ahead and ask, I might not answer it though."

"We know the presidential candidate is the head of the Ecru drug cartel. Since you are a New York City detective, and he was killed on the steps of your city hall, do you know who may be the culprit who shot him?"

A question like the one asked she will not give a reply. First, she is cognizant they no doubt are informed of the answer before they ask. Second, there is no way in hell she will ever admit to killing a presidential candidate. An experienced cop she has been around long enough to know there are no secrets. Someone, she doesn't remember who, in her past told her once your words leave your mouth you don't own them anymore. Third, her suspicions are aroused when a common tour guide knows all about her. In her mind, this woman is not an ordinary guide.

Ready to change the subject she responds with this answer.

"C'mon lets go eat, I think dinner is being served."

The elderly woman brings out some plates and sets them on the wooden table. The chairs are different styles, heights, and colors. For dinner, there are enchiladas with a rich sauce to dip them in. A gray cat wanders around the room waiting for food to be dropped onto the floor, otherwise is not a bother to anyone sitting and eating.

A two-liter bottle of Mexican red wine is opened and poured into short highball glasses.

The guide offers a toast to her guests and everyone starts to eat the meal. Afterwards, she announces they will be at their destination before nine in the morning. Continuing to speak the guide asks if there is anything the two women need please ask her, and she will try to obtain it for them.

"My superior said I should help you in any way I can. Please feel free to tell me how I can be of assistance. My orders come directly from higher-ups in Mexico City."

After dinner, Khara retires to her room, slips a plastic wedge she travels with under the door to prevent it from opening, and lies on the bed with her snub nose next to the pillow.

Chapter Thirteen

Before dawn, everyone in the house is up and thanking the elderly woman for her hospitality. Coffee is warming on the old iron stove, and Khara pours herself a cup. Now standing in the kitchen she can hear a dull beeping and glances up at the screen on the wall to heed two men walking in the courtyard.

"Olga, look up at the screen."

All the lights are turned off, and they are only bathed in shallow exterior light coming in through the windows.

Guns are drawn.

Khara walks to the front door and realizes it is unlocked. Last night before she went to bed she made sure all the doors are locked. Someone in the house had to open it after she went to sleep. With her gun at the ready, she stands to the side of the front entry door by the hinges.

In the meantime, Olga hustles to the rear door of the home. Both raise their head up, follow the men's movement on the screen, and can view each one is standing by a door. The cameras show each of them carries a weapon in their hand and can be seen reaching for the door handle. With eyes peeled on the monitor, they eyeball them twist the handle and start to open the doors.

Olga nods to Khara, and both women begin to shoot through the wooden doors. After a few shots, they each open a door and a man's body is sprawled on the dirt outside.

Khara kneels to place two fingers on the neck of the man by her door trying to find out if a pulse exists but cannot find one. Olga does not bother as she is standing over the man, and with a cursory glance checks to find out if there is a chest compression. None can be found.

The whole time the shooting is going on the Mexican guide is in the bathroom behind a locked door. After the shooting is over she opens the door and walks out seeing both women still alive.

Olga stands and stares at the woman, and asks her a question.

"How did these men know we are here? We were not followed because I checked as you drove. This is a safe house. Only you know where we were going to stay."

Like a deer in headlights, the woman froze and Olga raises her gun and aims it at the woman.

"They forced me to tell them. The colonel said he would rape and kill my young daughters. He is ruthless, I had no choice."

Khara stood and listened saying nothing. This, she thought to herself, is Olga's contact not hers.

"So you would kill us, and be on your way, right?"

The guide said nothing knowing she is dealing with two killers.

A shot rang out with a piercing echo off the tin roof in the small tiled wall kitchen.

"We'll need to drive ourselves Khara, let's go."

With their bags in their hands, both women step over the guide's body. Khara searches the woman's clothing until she finds the keys to the van, and they exit out the back door to the Nissan.

Khara inspects at the vehicle and is in doubt about using it to go to Nuevo Laredo. "I wouldn't be surprised if it is bugged, or a tracking device is hidden on it."

"You are right. What do you suggest we do now?"

"We are only a block or so off the state highway, and a bus or truck must be going our way. I'll ask the elderly woman."

Back inside Khara catches the old woman on the phone saying the two left the safe house after shooting the guide and taking her car. Now realizing she must be reporting to the Secret Police what happened in the house Khara stands in silence until the woman hangs up. She places the handset down and the elderly woman turns and is shocked to find out who is standing in the doorway.

Startled the woman grabs a polished steel chef's knife from the counter and attempts to run toward Khara limping as she moves forward. She grabs the old lady's wrist while she forces the knife backward, and plunges the blade into her chest. Twisting it from side to side blood starts to pour out of the old woman's mouth. Khara, with all her strength, pushes her away as she falls to the floor almost motionless.

Pissed at the turn of events she leaves the kitchen and walks over to Olga who is waiting outside.

"Both of those bitches were working for the Colonel. He is told by them we left the house so we might as well take the van anyway. Let him expect us, I have an idea for when we arrive, let's go."

The gate is opened by hand as the Nissan pulls out onto the street, and heads north to the highway. They pass San Marcos Mexico on the way to Nuevo Laredo when Khara lifts her eyes to see in the rearview mirror and is alarmed when a car is coming up fast behind them filled with men.

"Olga quick behind us a tan car is coming up fast. Get ready they are going to try to pass us."

Buckled in the rear seat Olga raises her skirt and withdraws the Glock from its leg holster. Khara presses the window buttons with her left hand while having her Sig Sauer in her right hand and all the glass in the front and rear of the van is lowered.

With her right foot stomping down on the gas pedal the van starts to go faster as the car behind them is catching up. There is no way the Nissan van can outrun its pursuer. The quicker it is going the more unstable it becomes on the winding roads in the middle of nowhere. A family vehicle is not a sports car nor is it intended to be used for a life and death automobile chase.

The pursuing vehicle is gaining on them and is now much closer and tailgating when Khara slams on the brakes. The driver of the car does not expect or is not prepared to stop as quick, and he smashes into the rear of the van. They are wearing seat belts so Olga and Khara feel the impact of the crash, but are not injured. In haste they are unbuckling the shoulder restraints, open the doors to the van, and scamper out towards the car armed and ready for action. The men are all bloodied, and appear to be woozy from the impact. Khara realizes they didn't snap their seat belts on. Two of the men who are sitting in the front seat dropped their pistols on the dashboard by the window when their heads hit it due to the impact. The men in the rear flew into the front of the car causing a pile of mangled bodies in the front seat.

     With guns drawn both women open the doors to the car, and in Spanish Khara orders them to step out of the car and lay down on the ground. The last man to exit the vehicle is somewhat hidden behind the one ahead of him and raises his gun. Olga is standing in front of the rear door and does not see him. Sharp-eyed and alert Khara does and fires off two shots sending him reeling back into the front of the car.

     "What do we do now Khara? Kill off these parasites?"

     "No don't waste your bullets. Watch them while I try to take the distributor cap from their engine compartment. The car won't run without it. A simple solution and it takes no time to do."

     In Spanish, Khara instructs the men to undress, give her their cell phones, and place their clothes in a pile on the ground while Olga collects their weapons. In their culture, to be dominated by a woman, and forced to undress in public is humiliating to these killers. It is done on purpose.

     Popping the hood open Khara reaches in and yanks the wires out of the distributor. With a quick twist, it is in her hands. While her head is under the hood she listens to two pops of a gun with a silencer on it. Not bothering to look she understood what Olga is doing.

Only a few minutes later, finished disabling the car Khara grabs all the clothes on the asphalt and throws them in the back of the van. Two of the gunmen are left lying naked on the highway. The one who drove the car is kept alive and taken with them, placed in the back of the van tied up using the pants from the dead men, and secured in the back with a seat belt.

"Let's go, Olga, we're finished here."

In Spanish, Khara speaks to the hostage.

"What is the address of the Colonel's safe house?"

"It is on Madero Street in Nuevo Laredo but I am not sure of the number. Do not worry I somewhat remember what the house is like, and how to get to the street."

Satisfied with the answer she feels he can at least take them close to the Colonel's safe house. Khara tries to remember what it looks like from the last time she was taken to the house. In a little while, they enter the city limits, and the gunman tells her where to turn street by street until they arrive on Madero Street.

The driver turns his head over to Khara and tells her it is only two blocks away after she makes a right turn at the next traffic light. Wary of the Colonel Khara stops on the side of the street and has their hostage call the Colonel on his cell phone.

"Tell him you are driving the grey van, will be at the house in ten minutes, and the women are tied up in the rear trunk area."

The driver dials the number and relates the message as instructed.

"Okay go ahead, and stop before you turn onto Madera Street."

In a short time, the van stops again Olga gets out with their bags. She finds a sprawling close to the ground bush and places their small luggage deep inside the underbrush. She is left holding a pair of pants from one of the naked gunmen with the sniper rifle hidden inside one of its legs.

Khara sits behind the driver and warns him not to stop until he gets in the driveway next to the house. "Stop when you are in front of the garage door, and not before. Remember I am sitting right behind you if you do anything foolish I will kill you where you sit."

The van restarts the final leg of the journey when Khara opens the side door all the way and tells him to slow down yet keep going. With the knowledge, life is expendable to the Colonel she does not trust any of them. Soon the van comes closer to the safe house when she slides over on the bench seat to be near the open sliding side door and places her right leg out of the vehicle.

Focused on the driveway the driver doesn't notice Khara slip out of the van. With a tuck and roll, she makes her way to the edge of the road and hides behind some dense growth scrub hedges in front of a row of residences.

About four homes from the safe house an RPG is fired from its roof, and the van explodes into a ball of fire. A secondary explosion comes from the gasoline tank being pierced by shards of hot metal. The van exploded and Khara used it as a diversion running into the rear yard behind a home, and into its barren backyard going from one yard to another until she is across the street in front of the Colonel's safe house.

A quick movement swinging the MP7 around on its strap she is now gripping it at waist level and running to the street. Secret Policemen come running out of the home to make sure no one survived the explosion. With several pulls of the trigger, each one is shot down in the street as she rushes to the right side of the safe house looking for the rear door. It is open, and Khara enters the home. The men inside are startled when she comes in, and they start to shoot at her. Ducking behind an old steel refrigerator she fires back but is unable to hit them.

The small pocketbook is swung around and opened as she decides to end this standoff, and takes out her hand grenade. The pin is pulled with her forefinger while shooting blind around the appliance to keep them at bay. She counts, flings the grenade towards the policemen, and runs out the back door of the house firing at them to give herself cover.

The explosion in the hallway of the kitchen sends shrapnel flying in every direction and penetrates a propane gas cylinder stored in the crawl space under the building. There is another blast, and the home lifts up off the foundation and crashes back down collapsing into itself and catching fire. Safely out of harm's way Khara is hidden behind the stone garage wall in the rear of the driveway.

The heat is searing but she is standing in a safe place when the garage door opens, and the Colonel walks out with a few of his men. Khara perceives they are yelling and realizes the garage is his hidden headquarters.

Raising her MP7 she is about to start shooting when a gun barrel is felt in the middle of her back. One of his security men is behind Khara and tells her to freeze or he will shoot. In the middle of her back, she can feel the barrel of a gun as she reels around, and smashes him in the face with her left elbow knocking his head into the stone wall. With a quick burst from the MP7, the guard slides to the ground as his legs give out. The Colonel and his men hear the gunshots behind them, now can see her, and start to shoot. The stone garage gives her some protection as she attempts to fire back. With bullets bouncing all over the place the Colonel realizes a few of his remaining men are falling to the ground all around him, but not from Khara's gun.

Coming up the driveway with her Glock spitting out flames of death Olga is shooting and hitting her targets. This gives Khara the opportunity to step out from behind the side of the garage, and direct her deadly MP7 shots to the remaining gunmen whose backs are now facing her.

Only the Colonel is left standing.

In Spanish Khara orders him to drop his weapon, and he complies. They are face to face.

"You know you will never leave Mexico alive Detective Bennet. What are you going to tell the police when they come here, and view all the dead policemen you killed? Are you going to now shoot an unarmed man detective?"

A shot is fired, and the back of the Colonel's head explodes throwing him forward onto the dirt of the driveway.

"No Colonel, but I will. Let's go Khara. You might not need to shoot him but I did. I'm through dealing with this dirtbag."

Both walk out and down the block to retrieve their bags from the bushes where Olga hid them. They start walking back to the main road away from the flames as fire trucks and police cars come screaming to what used to be a former safe house.

A car is passing by and Khara thumbs a ride for them to the border crossing. Two hundred American dollars is enough to sway the driver to accommodate them.

The car stops by the bridge to Laredo, and they step out to walk to the border crossing. The Mexican border police stop them, and both women show their diplomatic passports to the authorities. Khara, in Spanish, speaks to the officer in charge to find out if he can call the American side, and ask by name for the red-headed border guard she met last year when in Laredo.

In a short while, an American security vehicle comes to the middle of the crossing and waits for them to walk over to it, and climb in.

"A pleasure to meet you again Khara, I'm glad you made it back again. Do you have any spare time to spend with me, or are you and your friend flying back today?"

"What do you want to do Olga? If you need to fly back today I can stay here for a day or two. It's up to you?"

"No, I'll go back tonight if I can book a flight. You stay, and have an enjoyable time."

Soon they are back in the DHS Border Crossing office as Olga takes out her mobile phone, and online buys a ticket in first class. The border agent signs out for lunch and drives to the airport with Khara as company in his personal automobile.

Three days later Khara is also driven to the airport and is able to catch a return flight to Newark New Jersey. Viktor orders his limousine meet her when she lands, and bring her back to Brooklyn.

      ***

At last in her apartment, Khara unpacks and lies down on her king size bed to relax. The last week or so was a busy one for her. In a split second her head hits the pillow, her eyes closed, and her personal phone rings. The caller ID acknowledges it is Eloise calling.

Too tired to answer she lets it go to voicemail, and falls into a deep sleep.

Three hours later the phone rings again. Eyes half shut she leans over in bed and reads it is Johanna calling.

"Hello Johanna, what's up?"

"Are you back from Mexico yet?"

"I'm catching up on some sleep, I arrived late this morning."

"Yes, I thought you might be. Our sources at Homeland Security informed us the Colonel from the Mexican Secret Police has been killed along with a lot of his men. It is like every time you go to Mexico someone is dying. Would you say this is a mere coincidence?"

"Well it could be, why?"

"Late tonight the assistant to the Secretary of Homeland Security is flying into Newark and wants to meet you in my office about seven. Can you be here by seven o'clock, or do I need to send a car for you?"

"No need to send someone for me I can drive in. Of course, I still can drive the Corvette I borrowed from the security guard on Plum Island. How are the repairs to my M3 coming along?"

"Almost finished, the car should be ready later this week. I'll see you tonight, bye."

She stands, stretches, and walks in her kitchen to make a cup of black coffee. The clock on her television says it is almost three in the afternoon. Now is enough time for her to take a relaxing shower with her coconut body wash and spry on her favorite Chanel No.5 perfume after drying off.

Picking up her laundry from the hamper she tosses all her clothes from the trip to Mexico in the washing machine and starts to pick out her clothes for tonight. The new stretch blue jeans are selected along with a new white and blue plaid blouse to wear under a tight form fitting baby blue sweater over it.

This evening she will select a pair of brown boots from the bottom of her closet with a matching brown sheath for her knife. Instead of her favorite hand rubbed leather jacket a solid blue blazer is chosen.

After dressing she rearms herself, opens her dresser drawer, takes out a replacement grenade for her pocketbook, and with care she places her snub nose .38 in her right jacket pocket.

Everybody is cognizant how traffic at rush hour is in New York, so Khara calls downstairs to the concierge for the Corvette to be brought to the valet stand at five o'clock. In the meantime, she puts on a twenty-four hour news channel and sits drinking her coffee in the kitchen trying to catch up on the events of the day.

A few minutes before five Khara goes down to the lobby and the Corvette is waiting for her at the yellow valet line. The doorman opens the thick glass door with the deep acid etched mermaid on it for her, and the valet is standing in the street opening the driver's side door for her to enter.

Once seated behind the steering wheel she starts the engine, sits back listening to it purr and rumble, with the raw power pulsing through her body. Flipping on the radio Khara selects her personal mix from her phone as the Rolling Stones blast from the speakers and her Adrenalin races to every cell in her body.

Smashing the transmission into second she takes off heading to the battery tunnel. The trip goes about as she expected, slow. The Corvette exits in Manhattan as she turns and takes the city streets to One Police Plaza. The East River Drive is packed and slower this time of day.

The parking lot under the building is almost empty and finds no problem parking. Of course, she needs to go through the security tent first before she can enter the lobby to go upstairs to Johanna's office.

The elevator doors open, and two men in suits are waiting outside Johanna's office.

One of the men asks for her identification, and after showing it to them she is allowed to enter. Once inside other men and two women are in the outer office reading and waiting. The receptionist behind the desk recognizes her by now and waves for her to go into the inner office.

Johanna is sitting behind her desk and stands to introduce Khara to a balding gray-haired middle-aged man who is also in the room.

"Detective Khara Bennet I would like you to meet the First Deputy Assistant to the Secretary of Homeland Security Brock Jameson."

Khara decides to ask why he needed to meet with her tonight after pleasantries are exchanged.

"The Bureau of Immigration and Customs Enforcement, also known as ICE has been following the Ecru Cartel for some time. Because of their investigations, you came across their radar. Especially when you almost single-handedly eliminated them. The FBI and CIA also were dragged into following you because of your frequent trips to Mexico, and the mayhem which follows you on your trips. The different law enforcement agencies were instructed not to interfere with your travels. The directive came from the highest levels of our government. Sorry, but I cannot go into more detail than what I told you."

"One of our sources came across a picture of the late presidential candidate with an underage Mexican girl in the back of a car. We have reason to believe, although we cannot prove anything, you might be involved in the picture somehow. So all this brings me to the real reason I wanted to meet you tonight."

"This morning I spoke to your superior here, and I would like to transfer you to a new Federal Task Force I am starting. You possess unique skills we need, and you will report only to me, my close associates, and no one else. Homeland Security will move all your belongings to Virginia where we want to set up a house for you to live in while you are in Washington. Of course, there will be a significant increase in pay and a lot of travel both domestically and internationally. Are you interested?"

"What do you think Johanna?"

"Of course I will miss working with you Khara, but this transfer is for our national security, so I am in favor of it."

"Okay I'll go work for them, but I don't want to give up my apartment in Brooklyn. For continuity in my life, I need to stay in New York. This is my home base, and I have no problem traveling anywhere in the world for you."

"Khara we know all about your landlords and their deep connections to the KGB and Cuban Government. This is how one of our agencies also came across you. Over five different law enforcement departments are aware of you, and what you are capable of doing. Because of them, I selected you for this secret task force. Yes, you can keep the apartment if you wish it's not a problem for us."

"Fine when do I start?"

"I'll send a detail of aids to your apartment tomorrow to help you with your security clearance. The people I will be sending are my trusted agents and will be your go-to folks. How about we go for dinner and talk about a few things? There are other details I need to explain to you in private."

"Sure, let's go."

Being professional in an official meeting with Jameson Johanna comes out from behind her desk and shakes Khara's hand goodbye, and they all walk out of the office together.

Escorted by a small band of bodyguards Brock asks Khara where she would like to go for dinner. Being downtown, and the fact he is paying for it, she suggests a famous steakhouse near the New York Stock Exchange.

"Brock, why don't you come in my car with me and your men can follow? This way we can speak without others listening into our conversation. My car is not bugged, and your vehicle might be infected with listening devices installed without your knowledge."

Khara thought he is a little taken back by her thinking because she suspected he did not expect her to say what she said.

"Okay, I'll go with you. To be honest I'm impressed you thought of a bug in my car."

"You do have one in installed, correct?"

"Yes, but no one ever asked me the question before."

"There is always a first time for everything. Come on we want to go in the garage down below where I parked my borrowed car."

They are walking to the parked Corvette, and Brock views the sports car for the first time.

"This is a hot looking car Khara. How long did you borrow it for?"

"Only a few weeks so far, I loaned it from a terrorist I shot on Plum Island."

"Yes I read about the incident, and the shooting at his home. You do get around."

"Buckle up we're going to go for a little ride before dinner. There are a few questions I want to ask you in private."

The car pulls out and Brock's security team follows behind them. Alone in the Corvette Khara starts to ask him pointed questions.

"Tell me, and be honest, what this task force is about Brock, and keep in mind I don't have the patience for bullshit."

"Do you remember Colonel North and the Iran-Contra scandal under President Regan?"

"Somewhat I do."

"Going back to the era I mentioned we found a number of unsubstantiated rumors President Reagan authorized the flow of money and men to aid the Contras in Nicaragua. The task force I am setting up is similar to what he did, but more of an MI6 James Bond type operation. No gimmicks as in the movies, but there are assignments where your skill set will be needed. Please keep in mind I am not sending you out to be an assassin, but you might need to defend yourself with deadly force. My office can make you disappear out of any tight situation if needed in an instant. Your job would be to legally, if possible, correct situations where national security is involved. Other than what I said I cannot tell you more than I did. Every situation will be different. Are you still interested?"

"Of course I am. My shrink will tell you I thrive on excitement."

"Okay after dinner we can go to my office in the Federal building, and take care of a bit of the paperwork to move you over to the federal side of law enforcement."

"Two more things though Brock. First I hope you have a hearty appetite. Their steaks are fantastic. Second I want you to transfer my ex-fiancé, Don Weber, back to the city as a supervisor. He's in the FBI, and they transferred him to the Midwest somewhere. On the occasion when I come back to New York I want to be able to visit him. Hold on tight Brock there is a spot across the street."

Making a U-turn on two wheels the Corvette slides in sideways into the space with the centrifugal force slamming him into the door.

***

After leaving his office Khara calls Eloise and asks if she can stop by this evening.

"Of course you can. You know I would never say no to you. Would you like me to order some food in for you?"

"Don't order anything for me I ate a short while ago. I'll be there in a few minutes because I'm downtown and need to drive up to see you."

Pulling out of the garage at the Federal building she steers the Corvette uptown and parks in Eloise's parking garage. Living in the city Eloise doesn't own a vehicle but maintains a spot in her building for her clients and guests.

The doorman welcomes her and lets her in the lobby. The concierge waves to her but she doesn't stop to speak to him and continues walking to the elevators.

"Don't bother to call her she is aware I'm coming."

The elevator opens on Eloise's floor, and she is waiting by her door for Khara.

"Something must be important if you are here at night to consult with me, and not on a scheduled appointment."

The remark is ignored. "Glad you are better. How's the old ticker doing?"

"My cardiologist said I need to be careful for the next few weeks, but he does want me to exercise at a slow pace he said it is better for my heart.

"Guess this means I can't sleep over tonight?"

"He never said I can't-do sleepovers again. Now come in and sit next to me on the sofa. Tell me what is going on."

"The federal government recruited me for a secret task force. This assignment can be exciting, and also dangerous. In the past, I've been in situations like this before, and somehow came out okay."

"I know you can take care of yourself, but I still worry about you. Did they give you an assignment yet?"

"Yes, tomorrow a team of agents will clue me in on some details of what I will be doing. The team, I guess, they'll tell me in detail what is my first operation. The head of the task force told me tonight while at dinner in two days they want me to fly out on an assignment. Not sure what they need me to do, but I am to fly out to Berlin Germany. During dinner, I picked up bits and pieces about this American one-star general stationed at Anaheim and his aid. Not sure yet but I suspect I might need to stop an American insurrection. "

"Khara I'm tired. Come to my bedroom with me, and when we are in bed you can tell me all your thoughts on the first assignment."

"Okay but I want to shower first."

The End

www.CreativeFiction.net
Book 1 - Hot Cash/Cold Bodies
Book 2 - Khara Bennet - Vengeance
Book 3 - Dead Girls Don't Die

www.ingramcontent.com/pod-product-compliance
Lightning Source LLC
Chambersburg PA
CBHW060841280326
41934CB00007B/877